# 50
# northern california
# bicycle trips

By TOM A. MURPHY

with maps
By LINNEA RILEY

THE TOUCHSTONE PRESS
P.O. BOX 81
BEAVERTON, OREGON 97005

*Library of Congress Catalog
Card No.  72-89635*

*ISBN 0-911518-13-4*

# foreword

This book was written for the beginning and intermediate bicyclist who is searching for interesting and scenic rides in northern California. It is based on the idea that cyclists, especially those living in urban areas, will find a good deal more enjoyment in recreational cycling if they know where some of the really good trips are located. Many bicycle owners seem surprised that a multitude of quiet, safe, extremely enjoyable bike rides are within just a few minutes of some of northern California's busiest urban centers.

Most of the rides in the book are rural in nature and take place on some of California's less traveled back roads, while a few of the rides are found in some of the urban areas. The routes chosen on these more populated rides either follow officially recommended bike routes or carefully selected streets. A few of the rides, because of the road and traffic conditions, deserve special care and safety consciousness. This information is included in the individual trip description.

More than 900 miles of riding are represented in the 50 trips in this book. The average trip length is slightly more than 18 miles, with 11 trips under 10 miles in distance and 5 over 30 miles long. Each ride has been ridden, evaluated, altimetered and photographed by the author. Many beginning cyclists would undoubtedly consider some of the trips quite long while experienced touring and bicycle club enthusiasts would consider many very short.

The rides were taken from September of 1971 through May of 1972 and have been made as current as possible as of the date of this printing. However, conditions change. Cycling may be restricted in some areas (for example, on the 17 Mile Ride on the Monterey Peninsula), streets may change names, street signs may disappear or be turned 90 degrees for the sake of confusion, and roads may deteriorate due to weather or construction. It is the author's intention to revise this book periodically to keep abreast of changes that may occur. If you find any changes in the rides described in the book and want to help the author in the updating process, send your information to the author, care of The Touchstone Press, P.O. Box 81, Beaverton, Oregon 97005.

T.A.M.

San Jose, California
June, 1972

# contents

# contents

## acknowledgements

To Jim Brownson and Debbie Doerflinger who first discussed their ideas with me about a bicycle touring book and supplied information and support, I extend a sincere thanks.

To Linnea Riley of Ladera, California who gave of her busy days to produce in a relatively short period of time a beautiful collection of maps and elevation profiles, my genuine appreciation. Linnea's artistic insight into what was really necessary in making each map, her beautiful lettering, her ideas and consistent effort are much of the reason that this project has been possible.

Other friends have tested some of the rides and have offered their comments and suggestions too. To them I also extend my thanks.

And finally, to Kathie my wife, a very special thanks for her frank and helpful criticism, her proofreading, her companionship on many of the longer away-from-home trips, her forbearance and encouragement.

# How to Use This Book

This book is divided into four geographic sections. All of the sections are illustrated on a general northern California area map just before the trip texts begin and each section of the book is preceded by its own section map.

Section I covers San Francisco, the San Francisco Peninsula and the East Bay. Section II includes the north bay counties to as far north as Mendocino and Ft. Bragg. Section III extends from just south of San Jose to Carmel on the Monterey Peninsula, and Section IV encompasses the Sacramento Valley region, the Mother Lode and the Sierra.

*Maps*

The general map of northern California and the section maps indicate the relative position of each ride. These maps show the proximity of the rides to each other and the location of the rides with respect to major highways, cities and towns. These area maps are intended to be overview projections of the trip areas, and are not detailed and specific road maps. If you're not sure how to reach the start of some of the trips refer to an official road map of California.

Each trip map refers to the specific roadways on which the trip takes place. Cities, towns, parks, bodies of water and other landmarks and points of interest may also appear on each ride map. A START HERE label and arrow and directional arrows along the ride route always indicate where to begin and which way to go. More specific "where to start" information will be found in the first paragraph of the text of each trip (example: near the XYZ shopping center, just beyond the ABC golf course, ¼ mile north of the P and Z road intersection, etc.). Mileage information is also found on most of the trips (on some of the very short trips mileages have been excluded). These mileages can be very helpful in judging riding times and distances between important road junctions when you're cycling.

*Capsule Summary Information*

The heading information for each trip contains a capsule summary of the ride — its location, distance, riding time, where facilities are available and the ride difficulty rating. The general location information is intended to give you some idea of the area in which the trip takes place. Usually the cities, towns, parks and geographic areas described are familiar points of reference.

Distance information is self explanatory. Most rides are loops or circle rides while some go to and from a particular point. The mileage in either case is the total, completed ride distance.

The riding time listed in each capsule summary should be used as a guide only. Individual capabilities, equipment, weather conditions or just how you feel on any given day may have an influence on how long it takes you to complete the ride. The first time of the two times listed (example: 2 - 3 hours) is the more challenging but is still generally within the capability of an average cyclist in good condition. The second time is more conservative and approaches the maximum time it would take most riders to complete the trip. Please note that these times are *riding* times and *do not* include layovers, picnicking, or extended rest stops.

The Road/Traffic conditions are rated based on the following criteria:

**Road Conditions**

Good — Road surface may be smooth dirt or gravel or roughly paved or partly paved. Roadway could be rough, choppy or grooved in places. Roadway is usually narrow.

Very Good — Road surface is paved and smooth in most places. Roadway is wide enough or shoulder exists in most places to provide added cycling safety.

Excellent — Road surface paved in top condition. Wide shoulder or bike path exists.

Note: Rides on poor roads which might be damaging to equipment or which would be unsafe have not been selected.

**Traffic Conditions**

Light — Very little or no traffic. Motorized vehicle traffic danger is minimal or nonexistent.

Moderate — Average or moderate traffic flow. Cyclists should be cautious and alert.

Heavy — Ride takes place in urban areas on heavily traveled thoroughfares. Cyclists should be especially alert and use extreme caution.

Although most of the rides were chosen partly because of their favorable road and traffic conditions, some rides, almost unavoidably, have less than ideal conditions. On the routes with heavy traffic, conditions can be expected to become worse on holidays and busy weekends. Also, with the general increase in the volume of motorized vehicles on the roads today, traffic and road conditions will probably continue to worsen until, perhaps, we see the day that bicycling and public transit systems replace the automobile as the major method of transportation.

The term "Facilities" means the place or area where food, drink, restrooms, air for tires, etc. are available. It's sometimes nice to know on a longer ride away from civilization where these supply and service depots are. Most rides are suitable for picnicking. With the information provided about parks, picnic areas, ride distances and riding times you can plan a picnic layover in the location of your choice.

The ride difficulty ratings are one, two or three stars and signify an easy, intermediate or difficult ride. The ratings are based on the following criteria:

* Easy Ride. The ride length is less than 15 miles and the moderate terrain make this ride well within the reach of the cyclist in average physical condition.

** Intermediate Ride. With adequate time and some additional effort this ride is within the reach of the cyclist in average to good condition. Ride length is from 15 - 25 miles.

*** Difficult Ride. The length, terrain, and traffic conditions make this a more challenging ride. The cyclist should be in good physical condition and have some riding experience. Ride length is more than 25 miles.

There are 18 rides in this book that are one star or "Easy" rides, 26 which are two star "Intermediate" trips and six which are classified as "Difficult". It is recommended that you start by taking a few of the easy rides, especially if you're a novice rider or haven't ridden for a while. After becoming more at ease in handling your bike and gaining some physical stamina (your wind and legs) you'll be ready for some of the intermediate rides. Please remember that many of these intermediate or difficult rides can be abbreviated if you want to cycle in the area of the trip described and for one reason or another don't want to follow the entire route. The difficult rides are more challenging not only from the standpoint of total distance but also because the traffic may be heavier and the road conditions more diverse. These are the rides that should be attempted only after you feel you're in good enough condition to successfully complete them. Experience, stamina, "sticktoitiveness" and a sense of adventure are necessary ingredients for the longer distance cyclist.

# Safety

Any discussion of the fundamentals of recreational bicycling must begin with safety. And any discussion of bicycle safety begins with some very serious words of warning about bicycles and cars. Since the two use the same roadways and operate their vehicles under the same set of regulations, they theoretically should coexist as equals. Bicyclists, however, are less than equal on many counts when compared to automobiles or any road-operated motorized vehicle. For one thing, the sheer size and weight of a car and the metal protection around the driver make him a lot more secure than the cyclist. His vehicle weight at 1½ tons is about 100 times the weight of an average bicycle. The motorist also thinks in terms of cars and other motorized vehicles. When he is ready to pull out of a driveway or side road onto a busy thoroughfare, for example, he's looking for other faster moving vehicles, not the cyclist who may be happily, but slowly, pedaling along. When riding along roads with any volume of traffic it would be wise to remember this simple rule, and if you do, you'll probably be able to avoid any serious problems with motorized vehicles:

ALWAYS RIDE DEFENSIVELY. ANTICIPATE HAZARDS.

At times a motorist may just plain not see you. A combination of poor eyesight, road or traffic obstructions (like signs or parked cars) or poor visibility from within the car, sometimes may make you invisible to a driver. There are a few drivers who think the road belongs to them and only them. Cyclists are obstructions blocking their way and deserve no consideration or courtesy. These "nasty" drivers may even go out of their way to cut in front of you or ease you off the side of the road onto a soft shoulder. Luckily, though, occurrences such as these are very infrequent.

A cyclist experienced in touring becomes keenly aware of the conditions of a ride which might be potentially dangerous. He doesn't have to write them down or devote the first five minutes of each trip thinking about what to look out for, he just subconsciously tucks certain things in the back of his mind. Anticipation is probably the best word to describe the state of mind any cyclist should be in when he goes touring. Although anticipating hazardous situations becomes second nature to the experienced cyclist, the novice or intermediate sometimes doesn't realize he's in a pickle until its too late. The trick, of course, is to precondition yourself so that you will know what to look for and how to guard against troublesome conditions. Here are a few of the most common rules that cyclists should obey and things they should avoid and watch out for.

## Basic Cycling Safety Rules

* A bike, whether ridden by a child or an adult is subject to vehicle regulations. Obey all traffic signs and signals.
* Always ride as near the right hand side of the road as possible (not on the left as many cyclists seem to think).
* Try not to ride at night when visibility is poor. If you must ride at night use a headlamp and a rear reflector.
* Wear light colors at night and bright colors during the day. High visibility fluorescent gloves and vests are available to increase your chance of being seen.
* Don't carry passengers on the forward part of the bike.
* Try not to ride during or after storms when roads are slick and braking power is decreased (yours and motorized vehicles).
* Use arm signals for turns. Unless you are an experienced cyclist, walk your bike across busy intersections.
* Always keep your bike in good mechanical condition.
* Look ahead. Concentrate on the road and traffic in front of you, not on your bike or something to the side or rear. Many bike accidents, like running into a parked car, are caused by lack of attention to the roadway ahead.

## California Bike Laws

The following are California statutes and regulations affecting bicyclists, taken from Article 4 of Division 11 of the California Vehicle Code entitled "Operation of Bicycles". They pertain to everyone who owns and rides a bike.

1. Every person *riding a bicycle upon a highway, has all the rights,* and is *subject to all the duties* of the driver of an automobile. Some of these are stopping at stop signs, granting right of way to automobiles and pedestrians, stopping before crossing sidewalks, and stopping for "Stop" and "Go" lights.

2. No person shall operate a bicycle on a roadway unless it is equipped with a *brake which will enable the operator to make one braked wheel skid on dry, level, clean pavement.*

3. No person shall operate on the highway any bicycle equipped with handlebars so raised that the operator must elevate his hands *above the level of his shoulders* in order to grasp the normal steering grip area.

4. No person shall operate upon any highway a bicycle which has been modified or altered in such a way as to cause *the pedal in its lowermost position to be more than 12 inches above the ground.*

5. Every bicycle operated upon any highway *during darkness shall be equipped with a lamp emitting a white light visible from a distance of 300 feet* in front of the bicycle and *with a red reflector on the rear* of a type approved by the Department which shall be visible from a distance of 300 feet to the rear when directly in front of lawful upper beams of headlamps on a motor vehicle. *A lamp emitting a red light* visible from 300 feet to the rear may *be used in addition to the red reflector.*

6. Every person operating a bicycle upon a roadway shall ride *as near the right side of the roadway as practicable,* exercising due care when passing a standing vehicle or one proceeding in the same direction.

7. No person riding upon any *bicycle, coaster, roller skates, sled* or *toy vehicle* shall *attach the same or himself* to any *street car* or *vehicle* on the roadway.

8. A person propelling a bicycle shall not ride other than *upon or astride a permanent and regular seat attached* thereto.

9. No person operating a bicycle upon a highway shall permit any person to ride on the *handlebars.*

10. No person operating a bicycle shall *carry any packages,* bundle or article which prevents the operator from keeping at least *one hand upon the handlebars.*

In addition to these laws a new regulation has been added to require all new bikes sold to have reflectors put on both sides of each pedal. This is a very effective safety device because as the pedals move up and down the reflectors also move, calling special attention to the cyclist riding after dark. The same principal is used in the leg light which is more completely covered in the following section on EQUIPMENT.

The California Highway Patrol is enforcing laws regarding the carrying of bicycles on cars and campers. According to the law, bicycles should not obscure a driver's vision to the front (bikes carried on front bumper) and should not cover one or both of the brake and turn signal lights at the rear of the vehicle. Cycles that protrude past the fender line on the left side or more than 6 inches past the right fender line on housecars and other passenger vehicles are also in violation.

*Things to Avoid*
* heavy traffic on residential streets (if possible, take back roads, not main thoroughfares).
* riding bunched up; this not only may impede traffic but also increases the possibility of riders swerving into and becoming entangled with each other.
* running over sharp gravel, glass, wire or metal.
* riding in or turning sharply in loose gravel, sand or dirt.
* drainage grates with long slots and no protective cross members to prevent delicate bike tires, rims and spokes from falling through. (Getting a wheel stuck in a grate has been known to be damaging to both bike and rider.)

*Watch Out For:*
* parked cars pulling onto the roadway or vehicles approaching from a side road or driveway. Generally, these drivers are looking for other motor vehicles and may look right through the cyclist.
* motor vehicles making sharp right hand turns in front of you into driveways, parking lots or at intersections. Since vehicles moving in your direction may not see you, they may not signal as they turn to the right in front of you.

* motorists suddenly opening their doors on narrow, traffic-filled streets. If traffic is heavy try to stop and don't blindly pull out into the line of traffic. Anticipate door openers by glancing at parked cars to see if anyone is on the left side of the car.

* deep ruts or chuck holes in the road. Try to avoid them since they are damaging to rims and tires. Don't swerve carelessly into the line of traffic to avoid them.

* railroad or street car tracks which slant off diagonally. If you don't run over tracks at a right angle, you and your wheels may end up going the wrong direction.

* freshly tarred roads or melted road tar on a very hot day. It can really gum up your tires, rims and frame.

* flying bugs when breathing with an open mouth.

* ferocious dogs. Methods as to how to best cope with dogs that like to chase or bite cyclists are numerous. Some recommend saying a firm "No"; some say lay down in the street beside your bike and play dead; some say take evasive action (a U turn) or if you're going downhill, make a run for it. The best course of action to take beside sternly saying "No" and speeding up a bit is probably to grasp your tire pump (if you remembered to bring it) and make menacing gestures. Science can also come to the rescue in the form of an aerosol can of animal repellent (like those carried by postmen) or a very loud sounding little horn about 5″ tall and weighing 3 oz. The latter is also in an aerosol can and may be conveniently carried in a small rack attached to your bike. Most dogs, fortunately, are not vicious, and unless you're extremely afraid of dogs, the bicycle pump and stern language is the most economical, most effective way to deal with chasing canines.

On many of the rural rides described in this book you can trust your ears to alert you to approaching cars or trucks either in front or to the rear. If a car or truck is coming toward you and you hear or see another vehicle coming from the rear, there is a possibility that both may pass by you at the same time. In this kind of situation keep as far to the right as possible. If the car coming toward you is over the center line on your side of the road (getting ready to pass another car, for example) or if he's wandered across the line and again, a car from behind is likely to pass you and the oncoming car at the same time, be prepared to ride off onto the shoulder of the road.

When riding to the right along a line of cars backed up behind a motorist who is trying to turn left or who is stalled, be prepared for the driver who may pull out quickly to the right to go around the lineup.

When you're moving quickly down a steep hill make sure that you have control of your bike all of the time. Stay on your side of the road and be especially careful of loose gravel or dirt on curves. If you turn suddenly on this loose stuff, you could take a bad fall.

Undoubtedly, the best really "safe" cycling routes are the bike ways being built today. But like most things it is not possible to categorically endorse these routes. Some are very well designed for the cyclist's safety and convenience and some are not. Almost without question, the bikeways that are little paved roads, separate from public streets, with no motorized or horse traffic allowed are the safest and the best. Then there are the routes which have been established in some communities on city streets with lanes along the curb or lanes away from curbs adjacent to parked cars. They are clearly less safe but still usually preferable to no bike lane designations at all or just a hastily implanted sign along the road with "Bike Route" or a picture of a bike on it. Some of the bike lanes painted on streets far enough away from the curb so as to allow automobile parking should be approached with caution. When there are no parked cars the bike lane seems to hang out in the middle of the traffic subjecting cyclists, who think they are safe, to motorists who may disregard the painted bike lanes. On busy streets where there are parked cars, the cyclist must be as careful as ever of motorists pulling in or out of parking places, opening doors suddenly or disregarding bike lanes and driving in them. Suffice it to say that bike lanes or routes designated on public streets are usually better than nothing but they're no panacea. Still stay as far to the right as possible and don't assume you have immunity from danger just because you're riding between two white lines.

# Touring Tips

When you're cycling, just as when you go backpacking or hiking, you want to plan what you're going to take before you leave home. If a planned ride is fairly hilly and is near the beach, for example, you should consider taking along a water bottle or something to drink, some food if the next regularly scheduled meal is away from civilization, some warm clothing (for blustery beach weather), a few basic tools, a spare tire or tube or a patch kit, a pump, and a first aid kit. If you're getting a late start and there's even the slightest possibility that you might be riding in the dark be sure to take a light along. See the following section on equipment for specific recommendations. The list of things to take may seem extensive but remember that you're not lifting the few articles that you'll be taking with every step like a backpacker. Most or all of the loose items you'll be taking will fit nicely into a simple, inexpensive canvas or nylon knap sack, available at most bike or department stores.

## Clothing

Clothing can have a significant influence on how enjoyable (or unenjoyable) a ride will be. The following list and comments are experience-proven suggestions and start from the head down. In general, the longer the ride the more care should be directed to selecting these articles.

* short brimmed cap (canvas or waterproofed); should not be floppy or wide brimmed to obstruct vision.
* leather padded safety headgear. If you ride a lot, or even if you don't, you may want to invest in one of these.
* sunglasses (keeps dust out of your eyes too)
* light colored or bright shirt made of cotton or other materials which "breathe". Avoid shirts or jackets with wide or tall collars — they make excellent bug and bee catchers.
* pants or shorts which are comfortable, don't bind and don't have ridge-like inner seams (like jeans). Knit materials seem to be best. Special riding shorts or pants with a sewn-in chamois make for more comfortable cycling but can be quite expensive.
* lightweight socks (not nylon)
* comfortable sneakers or tennis shoes. For the more avid rider, shoes with cleats which fit into stirrups or toe clips and over pedals make for more efficient cycling.

Jackets should be bright colored, lightweight and water repellent. Wind breakers fit the bill quite nicely and are multipurpose for other sports and activities. High-visibility, light-weight, fluorescent vests are available in many bike shops and are especially well-suited for heavier traffic. Gloves are useful accessories which most experienced cyclists use regularly. They protect the hands from the cold, from reddening or blistering by rubbing against handlebars and from abrasions or lacerations if you should happen to fall. Official cycling gloves with open fingers (for coolness and to aid in handbrake operation) may be purchased in many bike shops. High-visibility fluorescent gloves are also available in some bike shops or from bicycle clubs.

## First Aid / Tool Kits

Packaged first aid kits and tool kits are available in bike and sporting goods stores, and many are very acceptable. (The Mafac brand tool kit is a good one and is small enough to be stored under your bicycle seat.) A less expensive alternative to buying a separate first aid kit and tool kit is to put together one of your own in a small box, leather pouch or plastic case. First aid components should include large band aids, a tube of antiseptic cream, two or so feet of adhesive tape and five or six 3″ x 3″ sterile gauze pads, a tin of aspirin, a few salt tablets, a tape-covered razor blade, needle, and a crushable ammonia inhalant. Although it may sound like a lot, this collection of first aid equipment is really very basic, and it forms a small, light package. A first aid kit of this sort is intended to relieve minor pains and injuries, like headaches and abrasions. These maladies are common among cyclists yet very few riders are prepared with any kind of first aid relief.

The tools and things that you select for your kit should include the following:
* a combination double ended bicycle wrench or small 6″ crescent wrench
* a small screw driver
* a spare tire (for sew ups), tube (for separate tube and tire clinchers) or a patch kit.

* an extra brake and derailleur cable
* a good pump

The trick in choosing tools to take along on any ride is not to take too much, which will weigh you down, create a bulky load, and probably never be used. Instead, as the list above suggests, take along the things you will most likely need and use. Also, if you keep your bike in good repair before you take a ride the likelihood of making on-the-road repairs is reduced.

## Riding in Groups

Riding with friends and family is becoming increasingly popular today. But group riding calls for additional awareness and coordination. The following guidelines are intended to promote safer, more enjoyable group cycling.

*Ride in a straight line* — don't weave or wander.

*Regroup* at the top of major hills so that slower riders can catch up.

*If you stop always give a warning by using hand signals or say you are stopping.*

*Before turning* look to the side and rear so you don't collide with or pull in front of anyone.

*Ride smoothly* and constantly; avoid intermittent speedups and slowdowns.

*Point out* or call out road hazards like holes, glass, grates and railroad tracks.

*Ride abreast* only when safe to do so. Riding more than two abreast is not safe. When a car approaches from the rear, the cyclist nearest to the shoulder should move up and the rider nearest to the road and traffic should slow and drop back into single file.

*When passing* other bikes let the rider know you're coming and which side you'll pass on.

*If you leave the group* let the ride leader know you're going or tell someone else who will communicate with the ride leader.

15

# Equipment

Good bike tripping depends in large part on good equipment. This doesn't necessarily mean expensive equipment. There are a lot of good buys today on new and used bicycles with acceptable frames and good accessory gear. Although it is not the purpose of this book to recommend specific kinds of bicycles to buy and equipment to use, some general observations about bicycling paraphernalia may be of some help to cyclists who are interested in touring. It should be noted that most of the bike trips described in this book are possible to take on almost any kind of bike in fairly good mechanical condition, from a one-speed to a ten-speed. There are certain advantages to cycling on a ten-speed, which will be pointed out below, but in this age of ten-speed mania, other lesser-geared bikes are still very effective. And if lots of good exercise is your goal, you'll certainly get more of it on a bike with fewer gears.

First, contrary to most reports, ten-speed bikes are not the only kind of two wheeled pedal vehicles made today. There are the one-speeds, which are usually fat-tired, big, and heavy, but dependable. Then there are the three-speeds which generally have a reliable cable and chain shifting mechanism and hand brakes. Like the one-speeds they are characterized by their weight and sturdy construction. Another type of bike is the collapsible 20 inch wheel three or four-speed which is now becoming popular because they are easily transportable and relatively easy to ride. Their convenience makes them especially popular with the older set who like the portability of this bike. Next is the continental five-speed which is just like a ten-speed except there is only one front sprocket or chain wheel instead of two. This means that you have five choices of gears in the back with the chain remaining on the one front sprocket. On a ten-speed with two front chain wheels or sprockets you have 2 x 5 or 10 choices of gears. For most people who are overwhelmed by five gear choices, a five-speed may seem more than adequate. However, with the additional front sprocket you'll get on a ten-speed you'll have a lot more gearing flexibility. Oftentimes, the second front sprocket is a small one and provides the gear range most suitable for hill climbing. This is a most important advantage. Also, the difference in price of the same make bike in five and 10-speed varieties is usually small. At any rate, a good five-speed is a little cheaper and has all of the attributes of a good 10-speed except gear range. That makes it a very acceptable piece of equipment.

A good ten-speed is the most ideal of all bikes when it comes to overall versatility and longer distance cycling. This is so for a number of reasons. Ten-speeds are usually lighter in weight than the one or three-speed bikes and they have a gear range allowing easier, more efficient hill climbing as well as faster cycling on level ground. These two features are the most important advantages of a ten-speed bike over any other, thus providing more miles of easier cycling than other bikes. Other helpful accessories are also easily adaptable or are standard equipment on ten-speeds. These accessories are things like center pull brakes for more positive stopping, toe clips or stirrups to increase your efficiency and keep your feet from slipping off the pedals, and quick release or wing nut hubs for ease in removing wheels and tires. It is also possible to increase your riding efficiency on a ten-speed by using a lightweight frame, featherweight handlebars and almost weightless aluminum alloy wheels and sewup tires. Although these accessories are more valuable to the avid cycle tourist or racer, it does point up the versatility and flexibility of the ten-speed. Bikes with even more than ten gears do exist, but they are not popular or widely used. The reason is that the added gear power does not offer much additional speed or hill climbing ability. In essence, more than ten gears are more trouble than they are worth.

The following summary of basic equipment and necessary or useful accessories is an overview of what one should look for in a ten-speed. There are also a few pointers on seat adjustment, what frame size you should choose, and what the proper handle bar and brake adjustments should be. This is not meant to be an exhaustive, in-depth review of equipment and cycle adjustments but rather some suggestions that could make your bicycle touring experiences more enjoyable.

    *Frames* — Double butted tubes (thicker walls at the ends than in the middle) are strong and light. Tubes which are put together with lugs rather than being welded tube to tube are usually stronger and better. Many welded tubes are in the lower quality/price range. Reynolds 531 and Columbus are the premium names in tubing materials. They're used in constructing the majority of the world's outstanding bike frames.

The right frame size for you can be roughly determined by straddling the top tube of the bike with both feet flat on the ground. If you clear the bar by an inch or less the frame size is about right for you. If you clear it by an inch or more it is too small and you will sacrifice pedaling efficiency unless the seat and handlebars are significantly raised (and this is sometimes difficult or impossible to do). If you can't straddle the top tube with both feet on the ground, the frame is too large and makes mounting and dismounting and pedaling difficult. For girl's bikes with no top tube this measurement is a little more difficult, but top tube position can be estimated and this method of frame sizing may still be used.

*Derailleurs* — A derailleur is the mechanism which makes your chain jump from gear to gear when the shift levers are pulled or pushed. There are many derailleurs on the market today and more being added all of the time. Two good ones are Campagnolo (Italian) and Sun Tour (Japanese). Campagnolo is an old name in bicycle equipment and is very reliable. Consult a reputable bike shop for further information on derailleurs.

*Brakes* — Center pull brakes are the best. They have a cable connected to the hand brake which pulls up at the center of the short cable stretched between the two arms of the brake. Center pulls give more positive, more even stopping power and cause brake pads to wear more evenly.

*Wheels* — There are basically two types of wheels you can get on a ten-speed and both have certain advantages.

Clincher rims are the most practical and economical. As the name suggests, tires on clinchers fit under a lip on the rim so that the tire grabs or clinches onto the rim as the air in the tube forces it out. Tires and tubes are separate and both are thicker and heavier than the one piece sew up tires. Rims are usually made from steel and are also sturdier and heavier than tubular rims. Although clinchers are a bit heavier and make riding a little tougher, they are less prone to flats, bent rims and untuned spokes — all in all a more practical alternative for the beginning-intermediate cyclist.

Tubular rims are very light and are dished on top to accommodate sew up tires (tubes sewn inside a lightweight tire). The advantage of tubulars and sewups is that they are extremely lightweight, which aids significantly in pedaling. The disadvantages are frequent flats which are difficult to repair, rims easily dented and flattened by bumps because of their light-weight construction and wheels and spokes going out of tune and needing adjustment.

Use recommended air pressures in tires whether they are clinchers or sew ups. It has been estimated that an underinflated tire traveling at 20 mph will require 30% more energy to propel than a tire correctly inflated. Clincher tire pressures range from 50 to 75 pounds depending on conditions and sewups take from 75 to 120 pounds under different conditions. Generally, the smoother and better the road surface, the more highly inflated your tires can be. Recommended pressures are usually written on the side of the tire.

*Seats* — Ten-speed seats are usually of the narrow, uncomfortable looking variety. The reason for this is that most ten-speed seats are designed for resting against as opposed to sitting on. The ten-speed cyclist with racing style, dropped handlebars, distributes his weight between his seat or saddle and his handlebars. He needs a seat which doesn't get in the way of his legs and doesn't bounce or spring and thus, absorb pedaling energy. The wide, spring seats are used mainly on bikes with regular flat handlebars where the cyclist is riding in a sitting-up position. Many girls' ten-speeds have the flat handlebar, wide spring seat feature. Try to pick a seat or saddle that sits comfortably, and try to imagine how it will feel after 20 miles or so. Steer away from buying the plastic molded seats being produced today. They are very cheap, hot, and very, very hard. Consider getting a good padded saddle for ten-speeds with dropped, racing type handlebars. They are available in most bike shops.

Seat height adjustment is a key to more comfortable, more efficient cycling. As a general rule the seat should be high enough so that your leg in the down position is almost straight. A more scientific determination of seat height can be made by taking your inside leg measurement from crotch to floor while standing erect and shoeless. Multiply this distance by 109% (1.09). The result will be your seat height, measured from the bottom of one pedal in the down position to the top of the seat. The pedal crank should be in the same line as the seat tube (the pipe in which the seat is inserted). This method of calculating seat height is based on extensive cycling efficiency studies at Londonborough University in England.

There are countless accessories you can hang on your bike if you have the money and don't mind the weight. Beside a small first aid/tool kit, a spare tube or sew up tire or a patch kit and a pump there are six other items which should be classified as *very desirable* if you plan to do much cycling at all. Items three and four are essential for night riding.

1. A rear view mirror — excellent safety device. It enables you to see to the rear without craning your neck around and weaving or possibly pulling into traffic or running off the road.

2. Toe clips — look like stirrups attached to pedals; prevent foot slippage, improve leverage and efficiency.

3. Leg Light — also known as a French arm band light. When cycling at night this handy little device can be strapped to your leg, above the calf and below the knee. As your leg moves up and down the light does too.  Drivers will notice this movement as opposed to a fixed light. It's red on the rear side, white in the front and some of them have a yellow middle light section. All three in combination are a good idea and provide front, rear and side visibility.

4. Rear reflector or pedal reflectors — either are good but pedal reflectors (attached to pedals) are the most effective. Like the leg light they move up and down making the night riding cyclist more noticeable.

5. A water bottle — to carry some liquid refreshment on longer trips. Some are made to hold hot and cold liquids. Attaches to bike frame in lightweight holder.

6. A lock — more on security devices below.

# Security Devices

Never have so many bikes been sold and ridden throughout the country as today and never have so many been stolen. In many areas stealing and reselling ten-speeds is a big business. Regardless of what kind of lock you may have, it is vulnerable. The 9/32" and 7/16" thick case hardened, cam alloy chains with strong padlocks with case hardened shackles (the U shaped part of the padlock) can be cut with bolt cutters just as the smaller chains and cable locks. The only difference is that the thicker chains and locks are more awesome looking and are more difficult to cut through. In many instances the sight of a thicker chain and the potential difficulty represented by a more substantial lock will discourage a would-be thief. After all, thieves are lazy. They are looking for the easiest bike to steal. There are so many bikes today that are left unlocked or with flimsy locks that the thief has relatively easy pickings. Again, large case hardened chains aren't burglar-proof, they're heavy and bulky and the good ones cost from $10 - $15. Like a good house lock though, these chains are just intended to make it more difficult for the thief.

An alternative to the sturdy chain locks which can weigh 3 - 4 pounds, is a clever little device called the Ryco Howler. It's a sound alarm that makes an awful screech when the cable is cut. Some sound alarms on the market are triggered when the bike is moved, but these devices are too sensitive to accidental movement. The Ryco lock is triggered only when the cable is cut. The locking cable attaches to a small case which contains the alarm horn and batteries. The case is permanently affixed to the bike and weighs about a pound. Like the chain locks, this device probably wouldn't stop the really determined thief, but it is a good deterrent and very likely would scare away the thief who has never called attention to himself while snipping chains with his bolt cutters. The Ryco lock is competitive in price with some of the more expensive chain locks. (See address section.)

Whatever security device you choose, remember that if you can park your bike within view and keep it locked you have a much greater likelihood of keeping it. Take your bike with you (even inside) whenever possible. And when locking up your bike, find a telephone pole, street sign, heavy bike rack or something else permanent which you can use as an anchor. A locked bike not attached to anything is as good as stolen. Avoid thin chain locks, thin cables (except for the stainless steel aircraft types which are quite good), the old shackle type bike locks and most combination locks. All are easily picked or broken by thieves.

Remember that once your bike is stolen you have very little chance of ever seeing it again. The registration and licensing systems operated on local levels are almost useless when it comes to recovering stolen bikes that may be transported to other counties or across the state. California is working on a statewide computerized registration and tracing system for stolen bikes but it may be difficult, even with this system, to recover stolen bikes. In summary, if your bike is valuable to you and you want to keep it, get a good burglar alarm lock or a heavy chain lock. The price is worth it.

# Bike Carriers

On some of the bike trips away from home you will want to drive to the starting point of the ride and carry your bike(s) along. A number of bicycle carriers can be used to transport one or more bikes. If you plan to transport your bicycle quite a bit, the purchase or do-it-yourself fabrication of a good rack is well worth it, particularly if you have a good bike that you want to take care of. Except for the collapsible twenty inch bikes which are built for trunk or back seat carrying, most bikes should be secured to a rack for long distance hauling. The reason for this is that bikes laying on their sides on top of a car, in a trunk or in a back seat are very susceptible to damage. Broken spokes, gouged paint and frames, bent rims and damaged derailleurs and brakes are likely to occur if your bike is transported without use of a bike rack. Your car can also become scratched and damaged.

There are three basic types of car racks for transporting bikes:

### Bumper-Type Carrier

This is the most common bike carrier and is characterized by two upright posts usually attached to the rear bumper. Hanger-type hooks protrude from a horizontal cross-piece stretched between the tops of the posts.

The rack is generally secured by metal hooks attached to the bumper. It should be equipped with straps which run from the horizontal cross-piece to the trunk lid or something secure on the rear portion of the car. Remember, according to the law, bikes and bike racks cannot block front or rear vision or brake and signal lights. Additional ties are used to secure the bike(s) to the rack itself.

The best kind of bumper rack will have hanger hooks with two dips into which the top tubes of two bikes can fit. The hooks should be covered by teflon or rubber. The good bumper type carriers are painted with a soft, protective teflon kind of material to help prevent rubbing and chipping your bike. The less expensive racks which look like they are chromed are susceptible to rusting badly. They are usually not sturdily built and will scratch your bike.

The advantages of this type of rack are that it is easy to "hang" the bikes on the rack, and it is relatively inexpensive. The primary disadvantage is that the rack only accommodates two bikes comfortably. When you hang your bike on this kind of rack make sure that bike tires or rims are not placed directly in back of hot exhaust pipes because the heat can ruin them.

### Car-Top Carriers

The main advantage of car top carriers, where the bikes stand up straight with wheels in the air are that more bikes can be carried. As many as six bikes can be transported on one of these carriers. Proponents of this kind of rack also claim less damage to the bikes since they are not strapped together and do not touch each other. If the handlebars are securely attached to the rack by U bolts and the seat is wedged in a V shaped bracket and tied in, the bikes will not bend over or fall off, even though their position looks precarious. This assumes, of course, that the ski rack type brackets are securely fastened to the roof gutters of the car.

The disadvantages of this rack (sometimes called the hernia bike carrier) are that it usually takes two people to lift, position, and attach each bike, it is expensive to buy and tricky to build yourself, and it is hazardous if you inadvertently drive into your garage or under a low hanging tree forgetting that the rack and bikes are on your roof.

### Lay-Down Trunk Carriers

For smaller cars, like sports cars, with spindly or nonexistent bumpers, the lay-down trunk carrier may be the only answer. This rack fits onto the trunk lid in a more or less horizontal position. It may cause bikes being carried to rub against and damage one another more than either the bumper or car-top carrier.

# Potpourri

Bicycles are no passing fad. They are here to stay not only as a sport and recreational activity but also as a major transportation method. In the town of Davis, California where there are 20,000 bikes for the town's 24,000 inhabitants, 47 percent of the businessmen and women own and use bikes for commuting. Some people who live too far away from work to bike all of the way drive part way to their jobs, park in an uncongested, free area and then ride their bikes the rest of the way. These auto-cyclists avoid some of the heaviest, most frustrating traffic, get good daily exercise and save money. With all of the bike lanes and bike ways being built today cycling will continue to grow as a viable method of transportation. But for the moment, cycling is primarily a form of recreation. The sheer growth in the number of people bicycling today will force city planners and lawmakers to give more consideration to the needs of bicyclists and provide suitable places for them to ride. We are already seeing this in several areas around the state. Beautiful areas like Yosemite Valley, where the automobile has seriously polluted the environment, are being turned back to pedestrians and bicyclists. This will enable visitors there to enjoy a more natural, smokeless and quiet Yosemite. Hopefully, other areas of beauty, like the 17 Mile Drive, will also see the light and, in the future, limit automobile traffic instead of bicycle traffic (see details in trip 35).

## Bicycle Clubs

Most bicycle clubs in northern California (there are more than 40) are dedicated to promoting safe, enjoyable cycling. Many also have helpful, informative newsletters from which you can get practical riding and repair tips. If you like riding places with a group on coordinated rides, you should definitely consider joining a bicycle club. Annual dues range from one to nine dollars depending on whether you take an individual or family membership. You should be careful when selecting a cycling club to join. Many are organized by and dedicated to the bicycle enthusiast who loves to rip off a century (100 mile trip) or double century (200 miles) on a lazy weekend, or who enjoys time trials and hill climbs. Most cyclists are not up to some of the longer, strenuous rides that the clubbers think are easy. Nothing is more disheartening than to find yourself in the middle of a group moving out smartly on a 50 mile trip when you know that you'll be lucky to make 25. Many clubs do provide what they call "sag wagons" on some of the longer trips to pick up the cyclists who, for one reason or another can't make it. Whether you ride individually or in a club try to work up to the distance you can most easily tolerate. Don't be overambitious and completely exhaust yourself on your first ride.

Names and addresses of all of the local bicycle clubs in northern California are available from the League of American Wheelmen (LAW). See the list which follows for addresses. The LAW is a national cycling organization promoting bicycle safety and dedicated to improving cycling conditions. The LAW puts out an interesting publication highlighting club activities, new ideas in cycling and repair and safety information. Individual memberships are $5, family memberships are $8. The LAW has been growing rapidly in membership in the last 7 years since its revival, still far away from the 40,000 members that the organization had in 1893.

## Litter

As you ride along some of the roads on the trips described in the book you'll be riding near or on the shoulder of the road and in clear view of some of the refuse that has been tossed out by passing motorists. Don't add to the glass, cans and paper. Keep California clean.

## Wine

Some of the rides described in the book feature wineries that are available for visitation and wine tasting tours. It should be emphasized that the wine should be tasted not guzzled. Since you'll be on your bike soon after your wine tasting, please remember that you have the same responsibilities as motorists. Don't drink too much and don't be a reckless rider.

## Ecology

Bikes are clean. They don't pollute the air with smog, they don't leave grease on the road, they don't make loud obnoxious sounds and they don't clutter junk yards with rusted rubble. Help promote bicycling by supporting bike ways, bike legislation and bike safety.

# MURPHY'S LAWS OF CYCLING

I   POSTERIOR COMFORT IS INVERSELY RELATED TO THE LENGTH OF THE RIDE.

II  ALTHOUGH ALL RIDES GO DOWNHILL AS MUCH AS THEY GO UP, IT WILL SEEM LIKE YOU'RE RIDING UPHILL MOST OF THE WAY.

III GIVEN A CONSTANT WIND DIRECTION AND VELOCITY ON A MULTI-DIRECTIONAL RIDE, THE WIND WILL ALWAYS BE BLOWING IN YOUR FACE.

IV  FLYING INSECTS ARE ALWAYS MOST ABUNDANT WHEN YOUR MOUTH IS OPEN.

**ADDRESSES**

*Bicycling Publications*
Bike World Magazine ($3/year) Primarily for intermediate - experienced riders or racers.
P.O. Box 366
Mountain View, Calif. 94040

Books About Bicycling (write for free catalog). Has all kinds of books about bicycling — touring, repair, history, etc.
P.O. Box 208-L
Nevada City, Calif. 95959

*Organizations*
League of American Wheelmen (Individual membership $5) Has a list of local clubs.
P.O. Box 3928
Torrance, Calif. 90510

*Security Devices*
Ryco Howler
One First St.
Los Altos, Calif. 94022

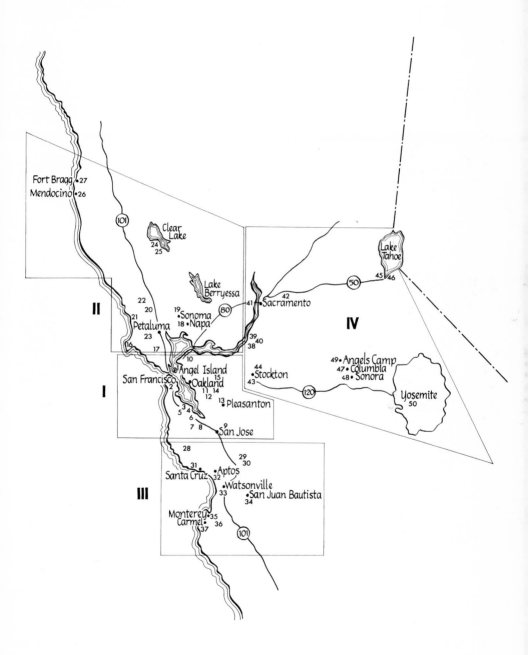

Fort Bragg •27
Mendocino •26

(101)

Clear
Lake
24
25

Lake
Berryessa

II

22
20

21
Petaluma
23

16      17

19
•Sonoma
18 •Napa

(80)

39
38

40

41 •Sacramento

42

(50)

Lake
Tahoe

45  46

IV

49 •Angels Camp
47 •Columbia
48 •Sonora

44
•Stockton
43

(120)

Yosemite
50

10

Angel Island

San Francisco
2

I

15
•Oakland
11  14
12

13 •Pleasanton

3 4
5

7  8

9
•San Jose

28

29
30

31
Santa Cruz
32
•Aptos

•Watsonville
33
•San Juan Bautista
34

III

Monterey •35
Carmel• 36
37

(101)

25

# 1  ANGEL ISLAND STATE PARK

**General Location: San Francisco Bay - Tiburon**
**Distance: 10 miles round trip**
**Riding Time: 2-3 hours plus ½ hour ferry time**
**Road/Traffic conditions: Very good/Excellent**
**Facilities: Tiburon; restrooms, picnicking -**
**   Angel Island**
**Ride rating: ***

*Trail along Richardson Bay*

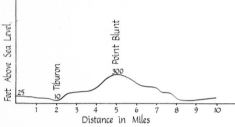

The starting point of this ride is on beautiful Richardson Bay near Belvedere and Tiburon. It can be most easily reached by taking Tiburon Blvd. (State Highway 131) east from U.S. 101. Approximately 1.5 miles from U.S. 101, Tiburon Blvd. passes Greenwood Beach Road on the right and the beginning of a delightful bikeway. The start of the bikeway marks the beginning of this trip.

The Angel Island tour offers some truly spectacular panoramic scenery to the cyclist. It is invigorating pedaling along beautiful Richardson Bay on the smooth, well-constructed Marin County bikeway which runs two miles to Tiburon. This bikeway is open only to bicycle and pedestrian traffic and it ends just before reaching downtown Tiburon. The views you will have on Angel Island are even more magnificent than on the Richardson Bay bikeway. The ferry ride to the island and the fact that there are no cars to compete with make this trip a unique experience.

The ferry to Angel Island leaves from the Tiburon Ferry Dock near the Windjammer on Tiburon's main street. There is a sign on the main street pointing down a narrow boardwalk toward the ferry dock. The round trip ticket for the Angel Island Ferry is $1.50 for adults and $.75 for children 5 to 14 years old. An additional $.25 for each bike may be charged. Admission to Angel Island State Park is $.25. The ride to Angel Island across Racoon Strait on the small ferry

boat is quite short and offers a spectacular bayside view of Tiburon, Sausalito and San Francisco. On the way you will undoubtedly pass many fishing boats, sailboats and motorized pleasure boats.

Start the trip on Angel Island by taking the road to the left of the main ranger building. You'll go by a picnic area and up a short steep hill before turning left on the main road. On this route you will see Bluff Point on the mainland north of Tiburon. Further on you'll pass by the "off limits" restricted area occupied mainly by deserted old military buildings and pass a dead end road leading down to Pt. Blunt (off limits). Many of the deserted buildings are in the process of being torn down or will be in the future. Upon leaving the restricted area you'll climb (or maybe walk) up a short steep hill and then work your way down the eastern side of the island past Knox Point and Stuart Point Light Stations. From this side of the island you will have an excellent view of the Berkeley Hills, Alcatraz Island, San Francisco and the Golden Gate Bridge. Although there are several paths leading away from the main road it's relatively easy to follow the route indicated on the map. If you have time, it's fun to explore some of the other trails. Most of them are suitable for bicycle travel.

Ayala Cove, on Angel Island, was named for Lt. Don Juan Manuel Ayala, captain of the first ship known to sail through the Golden Gate. Ayala anchored in the cove and used Angel Island as a base while he explored the Bay in 1775. Although his original naming of the island was Nuestra Senora de Los Angeles, it was later shortened to Isla de Los Angeles and finally anglicized to Angel Island. There are good picnic grounds, running water and restroom facilities in the area immediately surrounding Ayala Cove. The Park information headquarters is located here also.

Angel Island has had a colorful past. Under U.S. rule it has been an immigration station, a Public Health Service Quarantine Station, a fortified position for harbor defense, a military staging area during three wars, and a missile base. Although a small portion of land on the northeast side of the island is still controlled by the military and is "off limits" to civilians the Park will eventually include the entire island. All of the island's trees were removed by woodsmen in the 1850's, but many trees and other types of vegetation have since been planted by some of the island's inhabitants, making Angel Island today beautifully wooded and well-planted.

Please note the return trip ferry times before disembarking at Ayala Cove. The last ferry departure from Angel Island is usually posted on a small sign inside the ferry. Plan to reach the ferryboat dock on Ayala Cove about 15 minutes before its scheduled departure.

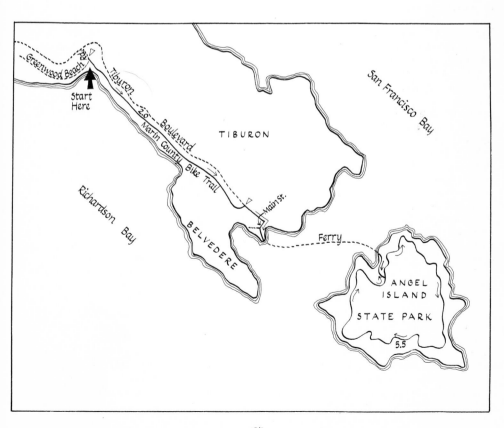

# 2 SAN FRANCISCO GOLDEN GATE PARK TO GOLDEN GATE BRIDGE

**General Location: San Francisco, Golden Gate Park**
**Distance: 14.6 miles**
**Riding time: 1½ - 2½ hours**
**Road/Traffic conditions: Very good/moderate**
**Facilities: Golden Gate Park**
**Ride Rating: ***

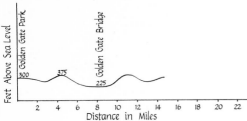

Bicycling in Golden Gate Park, especially on the weekends when many of the roads are closed to automobile traffic, is a popular pastime for San Francisco residents and visitors. Biking from the park to the northern end of the Golden Gate Bridge adds even another dimension to enjoyable, relatively safe city cycling. The route from the park follows official city routes (on 14th and Lake) and San Francisco Bicycle Coalition suggested routes (Arguello, Washington, and Lincoln). The ride winds through the Presidio where there are many spectacular views of San Francisco Bay and the ocean. Although there are some hills on this tour, they are short and only one, on Arguello, is quite steep.

A full day could be spent cycling in the park and relaxing or stopping and exploring some of the many points of interest there. John F. Kennedy Drive (closed to automobiles on Sundays) is a favorite pedaling route for cyclists of all ages. It has been estimated that 3,000 to 4,000 cyclists ride along this road on busy Sundays. Points of interest in the Park include:

- The De Young Memorial Museum — housing important art and historical collections.
- The Natural History Museum and Steinhart Aquarium across from the De Young Museum.
- The Japanese Tea Garden — an authentic reproduction; tea and cakes served.
- Morrison Planetarium

- The Prayer Book Cross (57 feet high) commemorating the first Christian service held in English on the Pacific Coast in 1579 by Sir Francis Drake's chaplain.
- The Dutch windmills (at western end of the park).

Golden Gate Park is a huge, carefully planned garden and offers something for nearly everyone. It is a fascinating place that has enthralled San Franciscans and visitors alike for many years. The park owes its existence and beauty to a Scotsman, John McLaren who was park superintendent from 1887 to 1943. The park was created from bare sand dunes in 1870 by McLaren, whose foresight and planning made the 1,013 acre park what it is today.

This ride route leaves the park and goes through the Presidio, once a garrison for Spanish soldiers protecting the mission. This heavily wooded, lofty area is today the headquarters of the Sixth Army and contains more than 1500 hilly acres. The reservation has been used for military purposes since 1776, when the first building was erected. Within the Presidio grounds is the Letterman Hospital for servicemen and their families and the cemetery which is the second largest national cemetery in the United States.

From the grounds of the Presidio, Lincoln Avenue leads to the Golden Gate Bridge. This huge, graceful structure was designed by Joseph B. Strauss in 1937 and built at a cost of $35,500,000. The bridge, illuminated at night by yellow sodium vapor lights, links Northern California to the peninsula of San Francisco. Two enormous steel towers, which you'll ride around, are set on concrete piers and act as props to hold up the giant "clothes line" cables from which the bridge is hung. These towers rise from the water to a height equivalent to a 65 story building. The center of the span clears the water by 220 feet. The western walkway side of the bridge is reserved for cyclists on weekends, and it is necessary to go through the tunnel underneath the bridge to reach this bikeway. Remember to keep right on this path so other cyclists may pass, and be wary of the strong winds, especially when going around the towers.

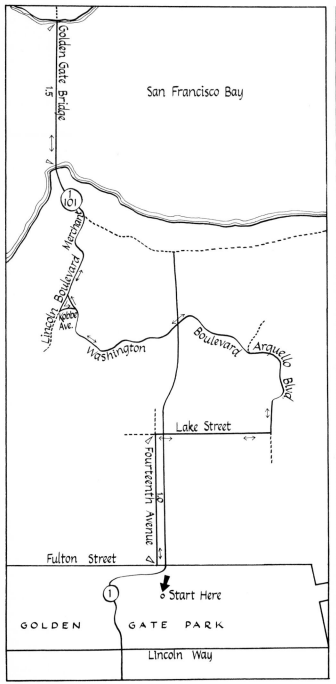

San Francisco Bay

Golden Gate Bridge

1.5

101

Merchant

Lincoln Boulevard

Kobbe Ave.

Washington

Boulevard

Arguello Blvd

Lake Street

Fourteenth Avenue

1.0

Fulton Street

1

Start Here

GOLDEN GATE PARK

Lincoln Way

*Golden Gate Bridge*

# 3 ATHERTON HOME TOUR

**General Location: San Francisco Peninsula - Menlo Park**
**Distance: 7.2 miles round trip**
**Riding time: 45 minutes - 1½ hours**
**Road/Traffic conditions: Very good/Moderate**
**Facilities: Menlo Park; Picnicking at Burgess Park**
**Ride rating: ***

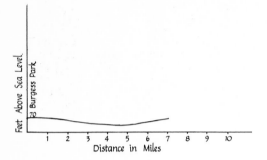

Feet Above Sea Level

To Burgess Park

Distance in Miles

Atherton is a fashionable residential area on the San Francisco Peninsula. This is a pleasant ride along some of Atherton's most beautiful, heavily shaded residential streets. The starting place for the ride is at Burgess Park, only a block north of El Camino Real off Ravenswood Avenue near the center of downtown Menlo Park. The Menlo city offices and library are located in this area.

Starting from Menlo Park (elevation 53′) this tour descends very gradually as you ride north toward the Bay. The roads you'll be traveling on are, for the most part, heavily wooded and offer ample shade. The impressive homes in the Atherton area make for interesting viewing. The large shade trees, gorgeous landscaping, and peacefulness of the area also make this ride extremely en-

joyable. Atherton was named after Faxon Dean Atherton, owner of the first large estate in the area established in 1860. Gertrude Atherton, the authoress, and Atherton's daughter-in-law also made her home here. The ride along this route offers a quiet, unhurried tour. It's a perfect way to get some moderate exercise and fresh air on a lazy weekend morning or afternoon in a pleasing environment.

The street markers in the Lindenwood part of Atherton are on low, narrow concrete pillars. They are difficult to see in some instances and you may have to refer to your map fairly often to make sure you're on the right street. Remember that you will be generally traveling in a seven mile clockwise loop on this trip and will return to the starting point via Willow Road.

*Gates to Lindenwood*

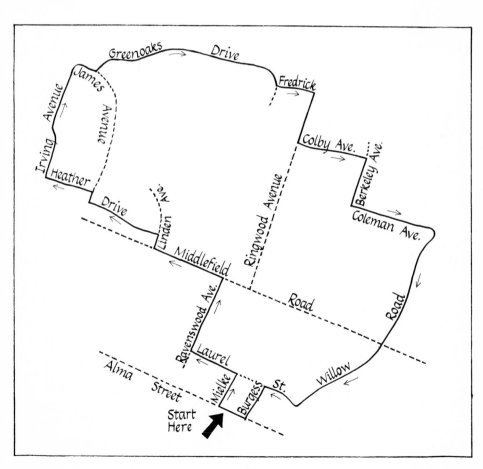

# 4 PORTOLA VALLEY — LADERA

**General location: San Francisco Peninsula - Menlo Park**
**Distance: 7.0 miles round trip**
**Riding time: 45 minutes - 1½ hours**
**Road/Traffic conditions: Very good/Moderate**
**Facilities: Ladera**
**Ride rating: ***

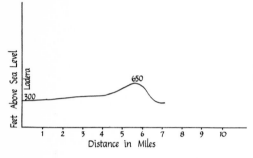

The little community of Ladera is located just south of Interstate Highway 280 on Alpine Road. The starting place of this ride is at the Ladera shopping center between La Cuesta and La Mesa Drives on Alpine Road.

This short tour has a variety of attributes. It offers a very good view of the Santa Clara Valley from upper Westridge Drive and an opportunity to admire some of the large interesting homes perched on stilts on the surrounding hills. You'll also be able to catch a glimpse of Felt Lake to the east which is not visible from the roads or freeways in the valley. By following this route you will climb Westridge then descends steeply before it terminates at Alpine Road. It's an exhilarating way to end the trip and a rewarding climax to your climb up Westridge Drive, which is a long incline, until it descends steeply before it terminates at Alpine Road. The pace down the hill is an exhilarating way to end the trip. This would make an ideal early morning or evening ride offering a varied terrain and interesting views.

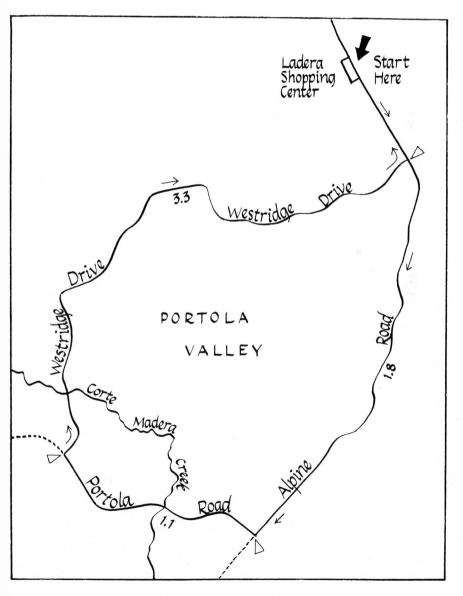

Ladera Shopping Center

Start Here

Westridge Drive

3.3

Drive

Westridge

PORTOLA
VALLEY

Corte

Madera

Creek

Portola

Road

Road

1.8

Alpine

1.1

# 5 WOODSIDE - PORTOLA VALLEY CIRCLE RIDE

**General location:** San Francisco Peninsula - Woodside
**Distance:** 14.5 miles round trip; Huddart Park side trip — 6.2 miles round trip
**Riding time:** 1 - 2½ hours
**Road/Traffic conditions:** Very good/Moderate
**Facilities:** Woodside
**Ride rating:** *

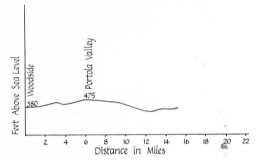

This circle tour begins at the junction of Woodside Road and Whiskey Hill Road in the town of Woodside. This point is most easily reached from Interstate 280 or Canada Road to the north, Sand Hill and Whiskey Hill Road to the southeast or State Highway 84 (Old County Road) to the west.

The Woodside-Portola Valley loop is quite flat and offers an outstanding view of the towering hills west of Woodside as well as Searsville Lake and the Stanford Linear Accelerator. Since this route is so convenient to Stanford University it is a popular ride, especially on weekends, for students, and older cyclists. The shoulder of the road for most of the way is quite wide and provides an extra margin of safety for the cyclist. In addition, near Ladera a paved bike trail runs along the right side of the road and continues intermittently to Alameda de las Pulgas.

The town of Woodside, where this trip begins, is small and quaint and is surrounded by a heavily-wooded residential area. The town has been created with a look reflecting the early days when the area was an important lumbering center. Old Woodside Store on Old County Road about a mile from the Canada Road - Woodside Road junction was the scene of much activity in the mid-1800's and is well worth a brief side trip. Established in 1854 by R. O. Tripp, the Woodside Store was once a post office and a food and liquor supply depot for the hundreds of lumberjacks that labored in the nearby redwood forests. Fifteen sawmills operated in the hills within 5 miles of the store, and the Woodside Store provided a gathering spot for these rough and ready men. The store is on the Huddart Park sidetrip, should you care to tackle a more challenging hill climb after completing the regular ride. Huddart Park can be reached by taking Old County Road west to Kings Mountain Road going north. The park is a San Mateo County Park which offers excellent picnicking and camping sites. The road to Huddart Park is twisting, steep, and narrow, however, and should be tried only by experienced riders.

The recommended loop should be well within most cyclists abilities and will offer a pleasant, scenic and refreshing trip. You will pass through a small portion of Stanford University property at the corner of Alpine Road and Junipero Serra Boulevard - Alameda de las Pulgas and will view a part of the lush, green, well-manicured Stanford golf course. The Stanford Linear Accelerator, a mile long structure, is separate from the rest of the Stanford campus and is located on Sand Hill Road going under Highway 280 and almost to Whiskey Hill Road, the return route to the starting point.

*Oaktree on Woodside-Portola Valley ride.*

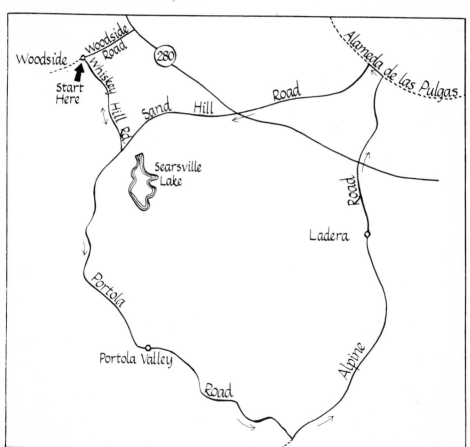

Woodside

Woodside Road

280

Start
Here

Whiskey Hill Rd.

Sand Hill

Road

Alameda de las Pulgas

Searsville
Lake

Road

Ladera

Portola

Portola Valley

Road

Alpine

# 6 FOOTHILL COLLEGE — LOS ALTOS HILLS RIDE

**General location: San Francisco Peninsula; Los Altos Hills**
**Distance: 7.6 miles round trip**
**Riding time: 1 hour**
**Road/Traffic conditions: Good (narrow in places)/Moderate**
**Facilities: Picnicking at Foothills Park (Palo Alto residents only)**
**Ride rating: ***

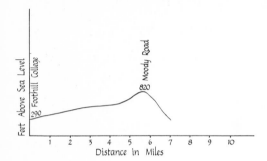

The parking lot at the main entrance to Foothill Junior College off El Monte Road is the pushing off place for this short circle tour through the Los Altos hills. Foothill College is just off the Junipero Serra Freeway (280) at the El Monte - Moody Road exit.

This ride will first take you along gently rolling Elena Road which parallels the Junipero Serra Freeway much of the way. Beginning on Black Mountain Road the route becomes more hilly until the high point on the trip is reached at the junction of Page Mill and Moody Road. Even though you will do some climbing before reaching the top of Moody Road this is a relatively short ride which is within the capabilities of most cyclists. The scenery is characterized by a mixture of fruit orchards and undeveloped acreage and ranch style homes. Many of these homes are large and beautiful and make for interesting viewing. For most of the way up to Moody Road the route is flanked by a bridle path. Plenty of horses and dogs may be seen in this part of Los Altos and Palo Alto Hills.

Although the road is quite narrow in most places on this ride, the traffic is usually light. The only area where the traffic is likely to be heavy is on the short section of Page Mill Road which you will follow between Altamont Road and Moody Road. Care should be taken here to keep as far right as possible. You should also be cautious when descending Moody Road. The grade is steep for about the first mile and the road is narrow. Check your brakes to see that they're in good working condition before starting down.

Besides the fruit orchards, the beautiful oaks and lovely homes, this ride has three noteworthy points of interest. The first is the slightly oriental architecture of the buildings on the handsome campus of Foothill Junior College. Established in 1958 this college has an outstanding academic reputation as well as being widely acclaimed for its attractive physical appearance. A side trip on your bike through the campus might be interesting. The jagged rock outcropping at the beginning of the ride adds an interesting flare to the oriental beauty of the campus. On Natoma Road you will pass Poor Clare's Monastery surrounded by a fruit tree orchard with an impressive gate and imposing building in the background. On Page Mill Road you will pass the entrance to the Foothills Park which is run by the city of Palo Alto. The Park has a wide expanse of green grass for relaxing, picnicking or kite flying, a little sailing and fishing lake and some hiking trails leading back into the hills. If you are a Palo Alto resident or are the guest of one, you are permitted entry into the park. Should you have the opportunity, the Park would be an ideal half way stopping point for a well-deserved rest or a picnic. Before taking the Moody Road downhill plunge back to the starting point at Foothill College you'll have a great chance to scan the scenery below in the valley. You may recognize many of the more noticeable land marks on the Stanford Campus, in Palo Alto, on Moffett Field or in San Jose. On a clear day you may be able to see San Francisco about 50 miles away.

*Starting point at Foothills College*

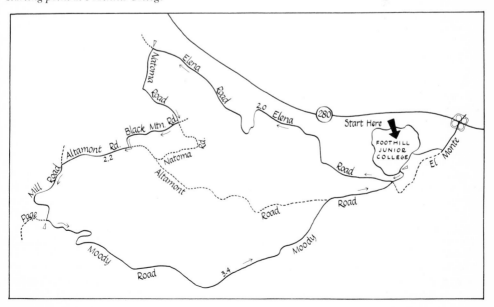

# 7 STEVENS CREEK PARK PICNIC RIDE

General location: South Bay; San Jose
Distance: 12 miles round trip
Riding time: 1 - 2½ hours
Road/Traffic conditions: Good; narrow in places/Moderate-heavy
Facilities: On Foothill Boulevard just before entering Stevens Creek Park
Ride rating: * *

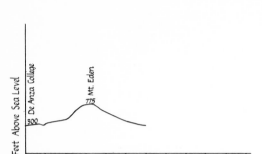

A parking lot area near the tennis courts at De Anza College in Cupertino is the designated starting place for this trip. This point, at the junction of McClellan and Stelling Roads, is one long block south of Stevens Creek Boulevard off Stelling Road.

Although this trip is less than 15 miles and would normally be classified as a one star, easy trip, it rates two stars because of the rather long, steep hill you must climb out of Stevens Creek Park toward Mt. Eden. Other than this challenging grade and the rolling descent on the other side, this ride is quite level. The view of the park, the blue hills of Saratoga to the west and the Santa Clara Valley are superb from atop the Mt. Eden Road.

Stevens Creek Park is a Santa Clara County recreational facility containing hiking trails, an excellent archery range, fishing and boating in Stevens Creek Reservoir and picnicking. If you decide to take this ride, plan a picnic at the same time. There are many delightful places along peaceful, clear, Stevens Creek to stop, relax and enjoy a lunch or just take a breather. The park is a favorite of South Bay residents who take full advantage of the facilities, especially on weekends. This, of course, poses some problems for the cyclist, who will have to contend with moderate to heavy traffic. So take care, especially from midday through late afternoon on weekends.

Once into the park, remember to turn left on Mt. Eden Road which branches left and climbs to the summit of the hill described earlier. Stevens Canyon Road goes straight and dead ends further up Stevens Creek Canyon. It is not recommended for cycling because it is narrow, steep and the traffic is fast.

From Prospect Road back to the start of the trip the ride route passes through a pleasant residential area and along a portion of the Cupertino Bikeway. The bikeway is indicated by signs along the road and bike lanes painted on the pavement. The bike lane "hangs" out in the middle of the street in places along Stelling Road to allow for automobile parking on the side of the street. It is not advisable to ride in the bike lane in those areas and think you are protected. Always stay as far to the right as possible even if it means not riding in the bike lane. You will find that some bike routes, especially those established in urban areas, are often less than acceptable. In fact, they sometimes represent more potential danger than nothing at all.

*Cycling through Stevens Creek Park*

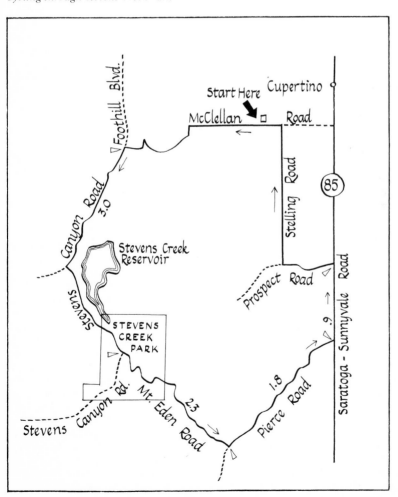

Foothill Blvd.

Start Here    Cupertino

McClellan  □  Road

Canyon Road  3.0

Stelling Road

85

Stevens Creek
Reservoir

Stevens

Prospect Road

Saratoga - Sunnyvale Road

STEVENS
CREEK
PARK

.9

1.8

Stevens Canyon Rd.  Mt. Eden Road  2.3

Pierce Road

# 8 SARATOGA — LOS GATOS NAVIGATOR'S DELIGHT

**General location: Greater San Jose - Saratoga, Los Gatos**
**Distance: 18 miles round trip**
**Riding time: 1½ - 2½ hours**
**Road/Traffic conditions: Very good/Moderate**
**Facilities: Saratoga, Los Gatos; picnicking in Vasona County Park**
**Ride Rating: * ***

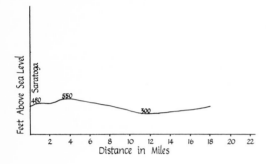

The pretty little town of Saratoga, nestled at the foot of the Santa Cruz Mountains, is the starting point of this trip. Saratoga can be reached from the north by State Highway 85 (Saratoga - Sunnyvale Road) or from the south by State Highway 9 (Los Gatos - Saratoga Road). Turn west in Saratoga on Big Basin Way and begin the trip at 6th and Big Basin Way in downtown Saratoga.

This circle tour follows many back roads through some extremely attractive residential sections of Saratoga and Los Gatos. These areas are characterized by beautiful homes, handsome landscaping, and huge shady trees along the route. On this trip you can avoid most of the busy streets and highways between Saratoga and Los Gatos while enjoying some of the more typical scenery between these two communities.

The town of Saratoga began as Mc-Carthysville in the mid 1800's. It was established by Martin McCarthy at the foot of the mountain toll road now known as Congress Springs Road. The name was changed in 1863 to Saratoga, because it was near a number of watering springs like famous Saratoga Springs in New York State. On this tour you will pass near the grounds of James Duval Phelan's Villa Montalvo. Senator Phelan first began to entertain guests, dignitaries, legislators, opera stars, and the literary elite at this mansion in 1914. After his death Senator Phelan bequeathed his villa to the San Francisco Art Association "for the development of art, music, literature and architecture in promising students." Villa Montalvo is open to the public.

From the area near Villa Montalvo the backroads of Saratoga take you to Los Gatos, another charming town. Los Gatos (The Cats) was so named because the heights above the town were once inhabited by mountain lions. Los Gatos is the home of Vasona County Park, a very popular picnicking, boating and general recreation area. A variety of row and sail boats are for rent on Vasona Lake and the expansive grassy areas surrounding the lake provide plenty of room for throwing a frisbee, playing ball or having a picnic. A refreshment stand and children's railroad are also attractions in the park.

The return trip from Vasona Park takes you through other parts of residential Los Gatos and Saratoga, past green, well-manicured La Rinconada Golf Course and near many of the striking buildings on the attractive campus of West Valley Junior College.

There are two short side trips for those who may be interested on this tour. In Los Gatos the Old Town Shops complex on University Avenue (see map) is a charming boutique center. Scores of shops and artisans' studios are neatly set in an old, redesigned red brick school building amongst several towering oak trees. And on Saratoga Avenue, less than one-half mile to the right (northeast) of the junction of Fruitvale and Saratoga Avenues, is the Paul Masson Champagnery and wine tasting room. The educational tour at the winery and the great variety of wines offered entertain thousands yearly.

*Vasona County Park*

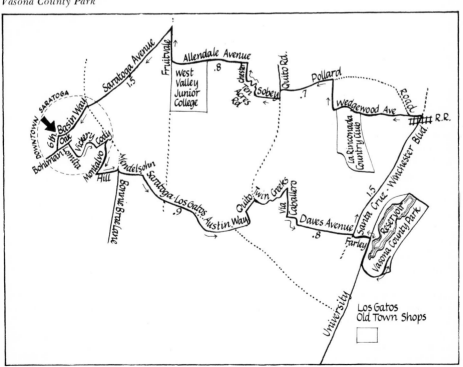

# 9 SAN FELIPE VALLEY

General location: East San Jose
Distance: 22.5 miles round trip; short alternate
   loop, 10.1 miles round trip
Riding time: 1½ - 3½ hours; alternate loop —
   1 - 2 hours
Road/Traffic conditions: Very good/Moderate
Facilities: At trip start
Ride rating: **; alternate — *

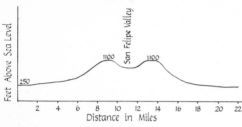

Only about 15 minutes by car east of
downtown San Jose in the shadow of
Mt. Hamilton is a quiet, picturesque and
pleasing country ride. The starting place
for this ride is in the little community of
Evergreen. To get there take U.S. Highway 101 south from San Jose to Capitol
Expressway. Turn east on Capitol to
Aborn Road and then turn right on
Aborn Road and go 1.2 miles to the
junction of White Road - San Felipe
Road and Aborn Road. A small shopping
center will be on your right and this is
the recommended start of the trip.

This trip starts with a very gentle 4
mile upward grade toward San Felipe
Valley and Shingle Valley to the southeast. At the junction of San Felipe Road
and Silver Creek Road you may choose
to either go straight on the longer ride
or turn right on Silver Creek Road and
take the short alternate return loop. On
the longer ride, you will pass Silver Creek
Road and begin climbing toward San
Felipe Valley. Most of the hills on this
portion of the ride are relatively short
but quite steep. You may find it necessary
or desirable to stop and rest periodically
or do some walking. The road is generally
"up" all the way to the end of San Felipe
Valley from the Silver Creek Road junction. In bicycling, however, what goes up
will come down (and vice versa), so, at
least, you can look forward to an enjoyable downhill coast on the return trip.

As you ride up San Felipe Road you
will smell the pungent odor of the large
eucalyptus trees. These beautiful trees
provide welcome shade on hot, sunny
days. Along San Felipe Road you will
see a variety of farm animals (cows, sheep,
pigs, geese) and as many as 25-50 black
tail deer grazing in fenced lands surrounding Rancho San Felipe, near the
end of San Felipe Road No. 2.

Metcalf Road turns right toward U.S.
Highway 101 and the town of Coyote
shortly before the Y in San Felipe Road,
but remember to keep left at this junction
as well as at the San Felipe Road Y, which
is only a short distance further. San
Felipe Road No. 2 takes you into the
heart of San Felipe Valley. Here you will
see some of the magnificent ranches that
occupy the valley as well as the San
Felipe Hills and Mt. Hamilton (4209') to
the northeast. San Felipe Road No. 2
terminates at the gates to the San Felipe
Ranch where you may wish to pause for
a while to enjoy the fresh air and magnificent valley view.

On the return trip be sure to turn left
onto Silver Creek Road for a delightful
alternate route, which, incidently, is
almost entirely down hill. This loop back
to the starting point is 6.1 miles and it
follows tiny Silver Creek most of the
way. The road and creek meander through
some very pretty rolling farmland. It is
authentic country cycling amazingly
near a large urban area.

Silver Creek Road crosses the Capitol
Expressway 4.8 miles from the San Felipe
- Silver Creek Road junction. Cross Capitol Expressway and proceed to Aborn
Road (remember that there is no bicycling on Santa Clara County express-
ways). Aborn Road, where you will turn
right, can be quite heavily traveled and
the pavement is rather narrow in places
so remember to keep right in single file.

A good idea after the conclusion of
this trip might be a picnic and wine
tasting side trip to small, quaint and
friendly Mirassou Vineyards on Aborn
Road. A visit to this old family vine-
yard and tasting room is informative
and extremely enjoyable. It is located
only .9 mile up Aborn Road from the
starting point of the trip.

   Winery Hours:
   10 to 5 Monday - Saturday
   12 to 4 Sunday
   Closed major holidays

*San Felipe Road No. 2*

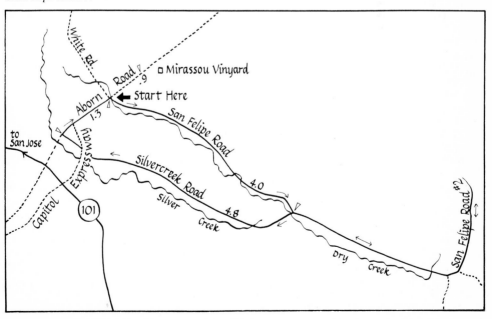

White Rd.

Aborn Road  .9  □ Mirassou Vinyard

◄ Start Here

1.3

San Felipe Road

to San Jose

Capitol Expressway

101

Silvercreek Road

Silver Creek

4.8

4.0

Dry Creek

San Felipe Road #2

# 10 SAN PABLO — BRIONES RESERVOIR LOOP

**General Location: East Bay - Orinda**
**Distance: 23.5 miles round trip**
**Riding time: 2 - 3 hours**
**Road/Traffic conditions: Very good/Moderate**
**Facilities: Orinda, Orinda Village**
**Ride rating: * ***

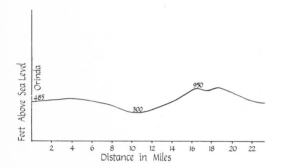

The San Pablo - Briones loop is an extremely pleasant ride through some rolling green farmland in northern Contra Costa County. The starting point for the trip is either at Orinda or Orinda Village which are adjacent to each other and only a mile apart. Orinda is located just south of State Freeway 24 which runs between Oakland and Walnut Creek. Orinda Village is a busy suburban shopping area and is just north of 24. This ride will first take you along moderately trafficked Camino Pablo flanked by a comfortable residential area and then along the shores of the blue waters of San Pablo Reservoir. The San Pablo Dam Road is more of a country road although it serves as a major thoroughfare between Pinole to the north and Orinda. Although the traffic moves quickly along this road, the shoulder is wide and provides a safe path.

The character of this trip changes markedly and becomes even more enjoyable after turning right (east) on Castro Ranch Road. The road is less heavily traveled and the countryside is dotted with small ranches, windmills, and grazing horses and cattle. People living in this area are avid horseback riders and as you go along Castro Ranch, Alhambra

and Bear Creek Roads, this will become increasingly evident. This land is gently rolling which not only makes for ideal horseback riding but also for great cycling. The only long, steep hill of any consequence is on Bear Creek Road, past the entrance to Briones Regional Park.

If you are interested in a picnic in the shade of huge oaks or an invigorating side trip up dirt and graveled Briones Road, stop at Briones Regional Park. Briones is one of the East Bay Regional Parks providing relaxing, scenic and recreational facilities for Easy Bay residents. Rough Briones Road, running through the park (closed to automobiles), climbs to the top of some high, treeless hills east of the park entrance.

From Briones Park Bear Creek Road ascends steeply to the top of some hills which offer an excellent view of the valley, Grizzly Peak to the east, and Briones Reservoir. As you coast quickly and effortlessly down the steep grade on Bear Creek Road you will pass beautiful Briones Reservoir far below you. At the bottom of the hill you will cross a bridge over the clear, rushing waters of Bear Creek shortly before reaching Camino Pablo to return to your starting point.

44

*Northern Contra Costa County*

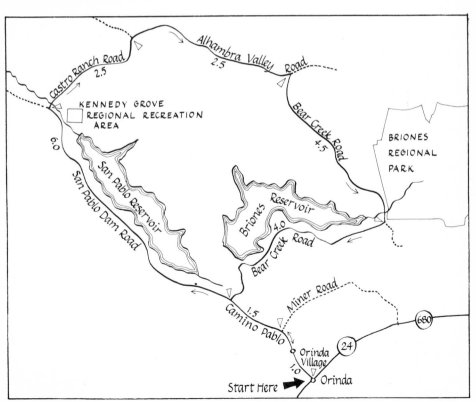

KENNEDY GROVE
REGIONAL RECREATION
AREA

Castro Ranch Road
2.5

Alhambra Valley Road
2.5

Bear Creek Road
4.5

BRIONES
REGIONAL
PARK

San Pablo Reservoir

6.0

San Pablo Dam Road

Briones Reservoir

4.0

Bear Creek Road

Camino Pablo
1.5

Miner Road

680

24

Orinda
Village

1.0

Start Here

Orinda

# 11 REDWOOD REGIONAL PARK

**General location: San Francisco East Bay**
**Distance: 13.5 miles round trip**
**Riding time: 1 - 2½ hours**
**Road/Traffic conditions: Fair/Moderate-heavy**
**Facilities: Shopping center at trip start**
**Ride rating: * ***

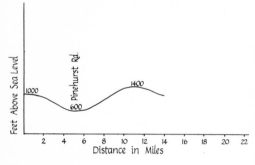

Redwood Regional Park and Anthony Chabot Park are located in Alameda County a few minutes east of Oakland. The starting location for this ride, on the western edge of Redwood Regional Park, is a small shopping center located at the junction of Redwood Road and Skyline Boulevard. The shopping center can be reached by taking the Warren Freeway (State Highway 13) to Redwood Road, or Interstate Freeway 580 south to 35th Avenue, which runs east to Redwood Road.

This is a relatively short trip but is rated as a two star ride because of the rather challenging hill you will encounter at the northern end of the park. Although this loop is a favorite spot for many avid bicyclists, the road is quite narrow in places and the traffic, especially on weekends, can be heavy. So be very cautious, alert and safety conscious on this loop.

From Pinehurst Road on the east side of the park you will have an excellent view of the upper San Leandro Reservoir as you speed down the long hill toward Canyon Road. On Skyline Boulevard on the west side of the park you'll have an outstanding panoramic view of Berkeley Hills, Oakland, San Francisco and the bay.

Redwood Regional Park is a part of the more than 8200 acres of land which the cities of Oakland, Berkeley, Piedmont, Albany, Alameda, Emeryville and San Leandro have set aside for recreational use. Redwood Regional Park, like most of the other East Bay Regional Parks, contains hiking and bridle trails, large groves of redwoods, deer, birds and other wildlife. Redwood Park contains some 2074 acres of unspoiled land and is designed primarily for daytime use. It is a quiet, green oasis in the growing, heavily populated suburban areas of the East Bay.

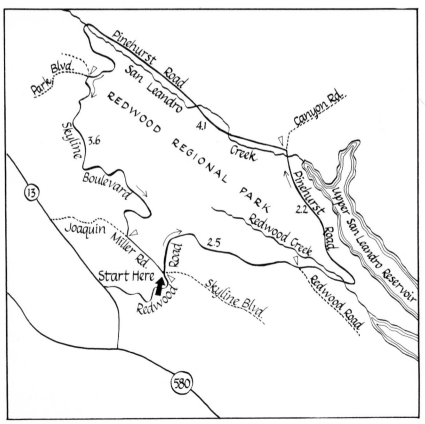

# 12 ANTHONY CHABOT REGIONAL PARK

General location: San Francisco East Bay
Distance: 11 miles
Riding time: 1 - 2 hours
Road/Traffic conditions: Good/Moderate
Facilities: Shopping center at trip start
Ride rating: *

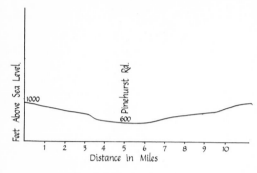

Anthony Chabot and Redwood Regional Parks are located side by side in the East Bay just a few minutes east of Oakland and San Leandro. Anthony Chabot is the bigger of the two regional parks and contains Lake Chabot at its southern end.

The starting point for the ride, a small shopping center, is located at the junction of Redwood Road and Skyline Boulevard. This point can be reached by taking the Warren Freeway (State Highway 13) to Redwood Road, or Interstate Freeway 580 to 35th Avenue which runs east into Redwood Road, or by following 35th Avenue east from Oakland.

This relatively short loop is rather hilly and slopes gradually downward from the starting point of the trip; down Skyline Boulevard, then down the fire road and finally down to the junction of Redwood Road and Pinehurst Road on the east side of the Park.

Please be sure to watch carefully for the unmarked fire road which goes to the left off Skyline Boulevard only 50-100 yards before Skyline Boulevard ends and Grass Valley Road (turning off to the right) begins. You will find the fire road just beyond a locked gate on which is a sign reading "No Parking". There are no motorized vehicles allowed on the road, so you will be able to enjoy a brief ride with no traffic problems. The fire road, partly paved, partly hard-packed dirt descends for about one mile before reaching a sign reading "Big Trees". Go to the right and up a short hill just after passing this sign and you will find yourself at the Big Trees Camp parking area. At this point, turn left (north) on Redwood Road and follow it back to the starting point.

Anthony Chabot Regional Park, along with its sister park to the north make up a part of 8200 acres of land which have been set aside for recreational use. The East Bay Regional Parks are operated by the cities of Oakland, Berkeley, Piedmont, Albany, Alameda, Emeryville and San Leandro. The parks contain many miles of bridle trails, hiking trails and hundreds of picnicking places in the many acres of unspoiled woods and fields. The parks are designed primarily for daytime use and overnight camping is not allowed.

Skyline Boulevard winds down a ridge which will offer you a gorgeous panorama of the bay and the cities of Oakland, Alameda and San Leandro to the west and the wide expanse of wooded and brush covered lands in Chabot Park to the east. On a clear day, you will be able to see the San Francisco skyline and the Golden Gate Bridge, and to the east, Mt. Diablo. There are several beautiful homes along the ridge on Skyline Boulevard which overlook the Bay and take full advantage of this superb view. Skyline is a wide, divided road (bridle trail in the middle) much of the way down toward the fire road which crosses Anthony Chabot Park. The traffic and road conditions on this part of the trip, therefore, are very favorable. Your route will become much narrower and steeper on the eastern side of the park, on Redwood Road. Care should be taken on Redwood Road to keep right and maintain control of your bike, especially down the steep grade on Redwood Road just after leaving the fire road.

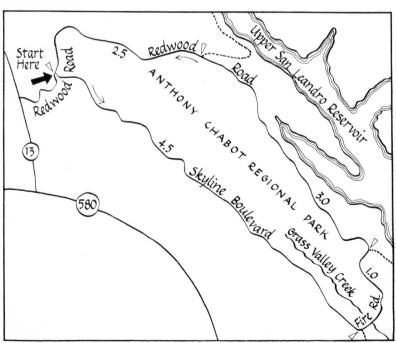

# 13 PLEASANTON RIDE

**General location: San Francisco East Bay - Livermore Valley**
**Distance: 24.1 miles round trip**
**Riding time: 2 - 3 hours**
**Road/Traffic conditions: Very good/Light; moderate in Pleasanton area**
**Facilities: Pleasanton**
**Ride rating: * ***

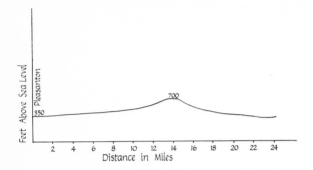

Freeway 680 is the most direct route to Pleasanton. The junction of Freeways 680 and 580 is only about 3.5 miles north of Pleasanton so easy access is provided from whatever direction you may come.

The general flavor of this ride is clearly indicated as you arrive in Pleasanton from Bernal Avenue. A large permanent sign stretches across the main street boldly spelling out "Pleasanton" as if to remind the visitor not to forget where he is. Pleasanton still projects the image of a small rural town even in the face of surrounding encroaching suburbia. Moreover, the ride route will pass through the heart of some lovely farming and ranching country — smooth and grassy rolling hills and cattle and sheep grazing on nearby slopes. You will first climb gently up Tassajara Road and when returning via Dougherty Road, you will undoubtedly enjoy the serenity and simple beauty of the area. The roads you will be on north of Freeway 580 are very

lightly trafficked and, therefore, are relatively safe for bicycle travel.

The community of Pleasanton is noted by horse trainers for the fine Alameda County Fair race track and conditioning track located nearby. Trainers from all around travel to Pleasanton to use this track which is reported to be the oldest horsetrack in California. Across the valley to the west just below Pleasanton Ridge is the Hearst Ranch, one of the first grand palatial estates owned by the Hearst family. It is maintained now as a private club and golf course. Each fall, La Fiesta del Vino, a wine festival, is held in Pleasanton. Many large wineries in the area are represented such as Wente, Concannon and Cresta Blanca.

Going north on Tassajara Road you will pass the Santa Rita Rehabilitation Center, now closed, and Camp Parks Regional Park, an Open Space area which has been set aside for future development.

*Ramshackle farmhouse near Pleasanton*

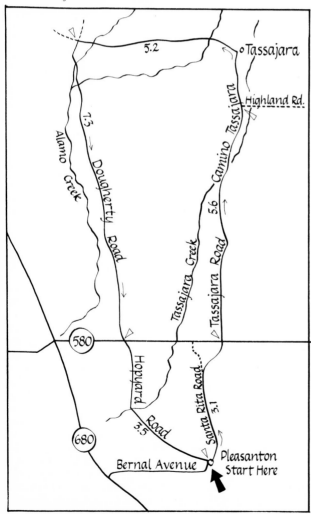

5.2

Tassajara

7.3

Highland Rd.

Alamo Creek

Dougherty Road

Camino Tassajara

5.6

Tassajara Creek

Tassajara Road

580

Hopyard Road

Santa Rita Road

3.1

680

3.5

Bernal Avenue

Pleasanton
Start Here

# 14 DANVILLE - DIABLO RIDE

**General location: San Francisco East Bay -**
**Livermore Valley**
**Distance: 10.5 miles round trip**
**Riding time: 1 - 2 hours**
**Road/Traffic conditions: Very good/Light -**
**Moderate**
**Facilities: Danville**
**Ride rating: ***

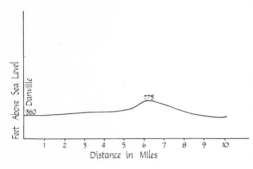

If you are looking for a short, scenic, easy ride in the Walnut Creek - Danville area, this must be the one. The route is relatively flat and is characterized by sheep and cattle grazing on the smooth grassy hills and purebred horses frolicking in the fields.

Little Danville is located between Walnut Creek and Pleasanton just off Interstate 680. To get there, take the Sycamore Valley Road turnoff west to San Ramon Valley Boulevard. Go north about a mile to Danville, then turn right at the first major intersection in Danville (Diablo Road). Stay on Diablo Road for about 3/4 of a mile to the Alpha Beta Center, which will be the pushing off point for this trip.

Danville, west of the Alpha Beta center and starting point of the trip, stands on land once owned by Daniel Inman, who first visited the area in 1852 and took up wheat farming in 1858. Danville sits in the shadow of Mt. Diablo to the east. The gate to Mt. Diablo State Park (2168 acres, open all year, camping, picnicking) is only 3.4 miles east of Danville. On the return loop of this trip, down Blackhawk Road, you will be very near the most outstanding feature in the park — the rugged twin-cone features of the 'Evil Spirit' or the 'Devil' — Mount Diablo. This grandiose, craggy peak rises alone to an altitude of 3,849 feet from a level plain and dominates the countryside for many miles.

Although a lofty mountain like Diablo so near a bicycle tour might indicate a hilly trip, this is not the case of this ride. Except for one short hill on Blackhawk Road, the Danville loop is a gradual up, gradual down jaunt. On the return trip on Blackhawk Road you'll pass the very impressive Blackhawk Ranch peeking out from behind an imposing heavy wrought iron and stone gate. Along Blackhawk Road you'll also see groves of walnut trees, usually with a black walnut trunk and grafted top. This area is horse country too, and you will certainly see a wide variety of beautiful horses in stables, in the fields or being trained in some of the horse rings in the area. After Blackhawk Road becomes Diablo Road shortly before returning to the starting point of the trip you will be coasting through some of Danville's most beautiful residential areas — sprawling ranch style homes with beautiful grounds.

Inland areas like the Sycamore Valley, in which Danville is located, can become quite warm in a midday summer sun, although early morning or late afternoon riding during the summer can be quite pleasant. In early spring the temperatures are mild and the softly rounded knolls on Tassajara and Blackhawk Roads are a beautiful, lush and velvety green.

*Danville Area*

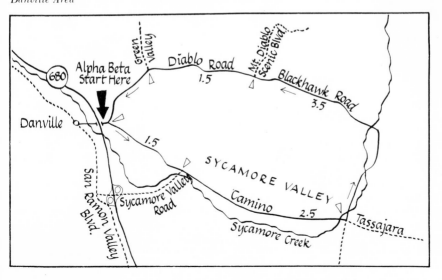

# 15 AROUND MOUNT DIABLO

**General location: Walnut Creek**
**Distance: 54 miles round trip**
**Riding time: 4 ½ - 8 hours**
**Road/Traffic conditions: Good - very good/Moderate**
**Facilities: Alamo, Walnut Creek, Clayton, Danville**
**Ride rating: ★★★**

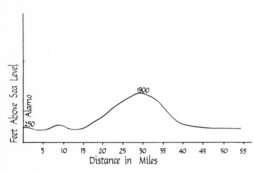

This is a long circle ride through some very beautiful country. The route you will be following circles Mount Diablo. The starting place for this ride is the village of Alamo, about 2.5 miles south of Walnut Creek off Interstate 680 (Stone Valley Road exit). From Alamo, you'll proceed north on Danville Boulevard to Newell Street in Walnut Creek. By turning right (east) on Newell, you'll miss some of the busy downtown Walnut Creek traffic. Please refer to the map.

This is a long, demanding ride which should be attempted only when you think you're in suitable condition. The ride is mostly flat from Alamo to the little town of Clayton but beginning on Marsh Creek Road, quite near Mount Diablo itself, you will begin climbing. You will climb more on the Morgan Territory Road (about 1500 feet in 11 miles).

Alamo, the starting point for the ride, was first settled in 1848 and 1849 when an adobe house was built among some thick groves of poplar, which once grew here. In 1854, two stores were built which drew their trade from the area's Spanish population. From Alamo, you'll ride toward Walnut Creek which in days past was an important shipping center for soft-shelled walnuts. Although many walnut orchards are still in the area, Walnut Creek is less oriented agriculturally today and is becoming a busy suburban bedroom community for the East Bay. You'll ride through the little town of Clayton just before reaching the Morgan Territory Road. Clayton is a small hamlet, although over 100 years ago it was prominent in California's coal mining boom. By 1902, soft coal mining had ended, partly because hard coal had been discovered in the Northwest. The town's small present population is supported largely by farming.

After turning right on Morgan Territory Road, you'll find yourself on a narrow, paved, almost traffic-free thoroughfare connecting Marsh Creek and Highland Roads. The Morgan Territory Road is perfect for cycling. It is peaceful, lush and green in spring and remarkably uncluttered by signs and housing developments. Cattle graze lazily on the grassy hillsides and quail hurry about on many parts of the 14.5 twisting miles of this road. Jeremiah Morgan laid claim to this territory in 1856 and used most of the land for cattle.

On the Morgan Territory Road you'll pass very near Mount Diablo. Diablo has long been known as a landmark as well as an outstanding vantage point. On a clear day from atop Diablo, you can see land in 35 surrounding counties and even Mount Shasta. Mount Diablo is located in a state park containing more than 2000 acres of land. According to Indian superstition, Mount Diablo was the resting place of Puy, an evil spirit or demon. The Spanish must have agreed with the Indian interpretation by naming the peak "Diablo" which is the Spanish equivalent of Puy.

The Morgan Territory Road descends steeply near its termination point on Highland Road. Make sure your brakes are working properly before going down. Once on Highland Road, the rest of the ride is relatively level through gently rolling countryside.

*Countryside near Mt. Diablo*

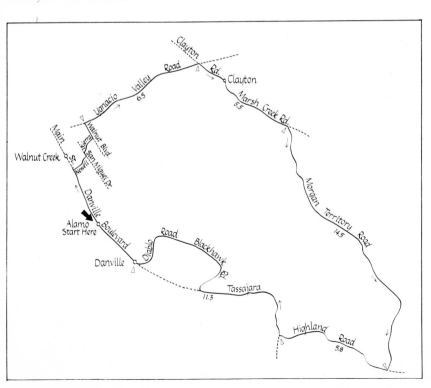

# 16 POINT REYES SEASHORE SALLY

**General location:** Marin County - Point Reyes Station, Olema
**Distance:** 40 miles maximum (may be shortened by starting at one of the Point Reyes beaches and cycling toward Drake's Beach or the light station)
**Riding time:** 3 - 5 hours
**Road/Traffic conditions:** G o o d / M o d e r a t e, heavy
**Facilities:** Point Reyes Station, Inverness
**Ride Rating:** * * * (For alternate, * family style ride, refer to final paragraph of this trip)

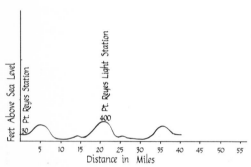

About an hour's drive north of the Golden Gate is Point Reyes National Seashore, one of the North Bay Counties' major recreational areas and a preserve of some of the region's most fascinating natural and historical points of interest. To reach the town of Point Reyes Station, take Sir Francis Drake Boulevard west from San Rafael to Olema, which is just two miles south of Point Reyes Station. Or, if you are coming along the coast, Point Reyes Station is on Coast Highway 1 at the southern end of Tomales Bay.

This ride can be as short or as long (maximum of about 40 miles) as you want to make it. The full trip down and back from Point Reyes Station has a few hills, so be ready for some climbing. As you pedal along, you'll have an opportunity to reflect on some of the area's colorful past.

Coast Miwok Indians flourished here in the 1500's along with a plentiful supply of wild game. Herds of hundreds of migrating elk and great flocks of water fowl lived in the area during these early years. Sir Francis Drake, for whom Drake's Estero and Drake's Bay were named, may have stopped here in 1570 to repair his vessel, the "Golden Hind," before starting out on his journey across the Pacific and around the world. Hard facts supporting this historical "maybe" cannot be substantiated, but there is a strong indication that Drake did stop here.

Many shipwrecks occurred along this section of the coast which ultimately resulted in the building of the Point Reyes Light Station in 1870. The light station today is a part of the land belonging to the U.S. Coast Guard and is not open to the public.

Geologically, Point Reyes has been separated from the mainland by the San Andreas Fault and during the 1906 earthquake, the peninsula moved, in places, some 15-20 feet. Tomales Bay, navigable by large commercial vessels in the 1800's, is today a sand and mud-choked inlet. Much of the land in the National Seashore is privately owned as it was in the days of early California, when several large Mexican cattle ranches occupied the peninsula.

The ocean has a strong influence on the weather at Point Reyes. Fog and wind, especially during the summer, make the area cool and blustery. You should bring warm clothing. Spring and autumn often bring the mildest, most pleasant days.

If you want to cycle in the Point Reyes National Seashore but desire a shorter ride, consider the trip on Bear Valley Trail starting at Park Headquarters (10 miles down and back). To get to the parking lot starting point, follow the signs to Point Reyes National Seashore in the small town of Olema. Follow the road to the parking area after turning into the Park Headquarters entrance. This delightful ride to the beach and back would make a good family ride. Motorized vehicles are not allowed on the trail, and the shady trip through the lush green fern and tree covered hills is very pleasant. At the end of the ride is a beautiful beach. The only thing to be careful of on this trip is losing control of your bike on the dirt and gravel trail.

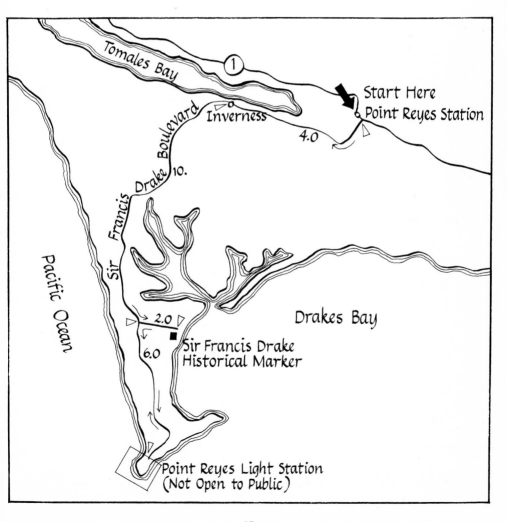

Tomales Bay

①

Start Here
Point Reyes Station

Inverness

4.0

Sir Francis Drake Boulevard

10.

Pacific Ocean

Drakes Bay

2.0

Sir Francis Drake
Historical Marker

6.0

Point Reyes Light Station
(Not Open to Public)

# 17 SAN GERONIMO - NICASIO RESERVOIR LOOP

**General location: Marin County between San Rafael and Pt. Reyes**
**Distance: 21.4 miles round trip**
**Riding time: 1½ - 3 hours**
**Road/Traffic conditions: Good/Moderate**
**Facilities: San Geronimo, Lagunitas, Forest Knolls**
**Ride Rating: \*\***

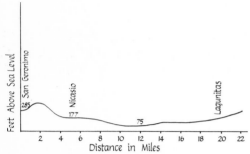

Marin County has some extremely beautiful places for bicycling and the area surrounding San Geronimo is no exception. Tiny San Geronimo is adjacent to the San Geronimo National Golf Course on Sir Francis Drake Boulevard. This little community is west of San Rafael on U.S. 101, and is east of the town of Olema on Coast Highway 1.

As this tour unfolds, you'll be exposed to a wide variety of scenery. To start off, you'll be climbing a rather steep but short hill north past the San Geronimo Golf Course and just to the left of 789' Nicasio Hill. From here until you reach the little village of Nicasio, the countryside is quite hilly and wooded in places with giant, wind-twisted live oaks and occasional green lichen-covered rock outcroppings.

From Nicasio, whose only place of business seems to be a restaurant, the land becomes much flatter and much more arid looking. Nicasio Reservoir looks like an oasis in a wasteland with dark mountains looming forebodingly in the background. Black Mountain (1280') stands immediately west of the reservoir.

The scenery changes again after reaching the Platform Bridge Road. On this leg of the journey you will gradually begin climbing along Lagunitas Creek toward Samuel P. Taylor State Park. Long-time residents of the area still call the State Park "Camp Taylor" because, for many years before it became a park, the area was used as a camping and picnic ground. The site of the present park headquarters, in fact, was once a hotel and tent city in the 1880's. Paper Mill Creek, which runs through the park, gets its name from the paper mill Samuel P. Taylor built in 1856. It was the first mill in the west and Taylor produced his paper from rags collected in San Francisco by the Chinese. There are several places along the creek in the park for wading and splashing, one deep hole for swimming, and numerous hiking trails. The dense stands of giant redwood block out the sun, making Sir Francis Drake Boulevard a cool, damp and darkened route. In the park along Sir Francis Drake you will see numerous picnicking spots, should you care to stop, relax, and enjoy the tranquility of the beautiful forest.

From the park it is only a short distance back to San Geronimo through the small communities of Lagunitas and Forest Knolls.

*Lake at San Geronimo*

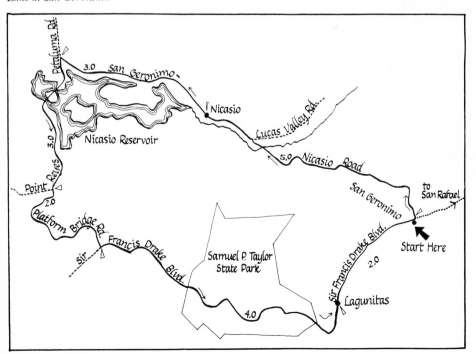

# 18

### NAPA VALLEY VINO TURISMO

**General location: North Bay - Napa**
**Distance: Open; Choose your own route from the suggested starting point. Maximum of 40 + miles round trip.**
**Riding time: Figure 8 - 15 m.p.h. on the route you choose plus stopover time.**
**Road/Traffic conditions: Very good; wide shoulder on most portions of Silverado Trail/Moderate**
**Facilities: Yountville and other towns on State Highway 29**
**Ride Rating: * ___ *** depending on route chosen**

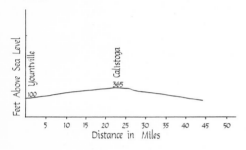

The starting point of this trip is tiny Yountville, which is about 8 miles north of Napa on State Highway 29. By beginning your trip at Yountville and using the Silverado Trail to travel up the Napa Valley you will not only find a more peaceful, less commercialized route but also a much safer, less heavily trafficked road than Highway 29. As you will see, the Napa Valley is quite narrow thus enabling the cyclist using the Silverado Trail to gain easy access to the Highway 29 side of the valley. The valley crossroads are closely spaced and are short in distance (maximum cross road mileage is only 2.8 miles). They provide easy access to the towns, wineries and parks on Highway 29. At Yountville, the recommended starting point of this trip, it is best to take Yount Street northwest to the Yountville Cross Road to reach the Silverado Trail on the eastern side of the valley.

Napa and Sonoma Counties are the backbone of the northern California wine-making districts. Most of California's premium wineries are located in these two northbay counties. Their origins date back to the early 1800's and the mission vineyards which helped establish California as a major wine producing state. The months of September and early October are probably the most active in the beautiful Napa Valley. It is during this time that the freshly picked grapes are crushed and placed in vats or barrels for the initial fermenting process of the new year's wines. The unmistakable pungent odor of newly crushed grapes fills the warm valley air during this time. Grapes are busily transported from vineyards to wineries for crushing and give the valley a certain aire of industry and excitement. Inside the wineries, guides and wine tasters still carry on touring and tasting as usual.

Yountville now stands on the southern portion of what was once the 11,814 acre Rancho Caymus, owned by North Carolinan George C. Yount. Two miles north of the town Yount built the first non-Indian habitation in the Napa Valley. Also at Yountville on the western side of Highway 29 is a large veterans' home. War veterans have been cared for here since 1881 when the home was first opened to care for disabled veterans of the Mexican War and Grand Army of the Republic.

The town of St. Helena is the next major town north of Yountville. Most of the large wine producers are located around St. Helena (see map). In fact, there are 14 wineries inside the limits of St. Helena and 28 within a radius of 6 miles. Most of these wineries in and around St. Helena are open to the public for tours and tasting.

Calistoga is the northernmost town on the trip. It was called Colaynomo or oven place by early Indians because of its underground hot springs. Samuel Brannan settled in Calistoga in 1859 and built a hotel and 20 cottages in anticipation of developing a popular health and vacation spa for early settlers. The name Calistoga is a combination of the words California and Saratoga (Saratoga being taken from the spa of Saratoga Springs, N.Y., long famous for its hot springs).

For those wanting to picnic or considering overnight camping in the Napa Valley, the Bothe-Napa Valley State Park is located at the junction of Bale Lane and Highway 29 near St. Helena. Since there are a great many places to bicycle in the Napa Valley, you may want to consider overnight camping at the park and additional touring.

*Inglenook Winery near Oakville*

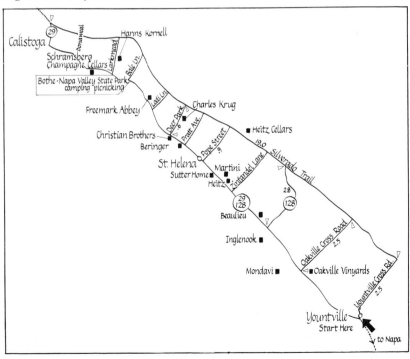

# 19 VALLEY OF THE MOON RIDE

**General location: Sonoma, Sonoma County**
**Distance: 18.3 miles round trip**
**Riding time: 1½ - 2½**
**Road/Traffic conditions: Very good/Moderate**
**Facilities: Sonoma, Boyes Springs, Glen Ellen,**
**    El Verano; picnicking at Jack London His-**
**    torical State Park**
**Ride Rating: ★★**

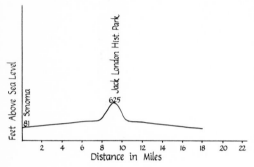

Jack London's "Valley of the Moon" provides a beautiful setting for this very enjoyable ride. To reach Sonoma from the west take U.S. 101 to Novato. Go east on State Highway 37 toward Napa and Sonoma, then turn north or left on State Highway 121 and left or north again on State 12, which goes into Sonoma. From the east take State Highway 12-121 west from Napa turning right or north on State Highway 12 to Sonoma.

This ride should start at or near the town square in Sonoma. From the square go west on West Napa Street (refer to the map). The ride to Glen Ellen is a very gentle upward grade. The only hill of any consequence on the entire trip is the rather steep one mile long grade from Glen Ellen to Jack London Historical Park. Unless you're a strong rider and/or have a good alpine gear you may feel like doing a little walking.

The main point of interest on this tour in Jack London's "Valley of the Moon" is a visit to the Jack London Historical Park. In this state-operated park you will have a chance to see an excellent

museum containing many of London's personal belongings. His grave site and the ruins of his grand residence, the Wolf House, are nearby. The major points of interest in the park are the House of the Happy Walls, where Charmian London, Jack London's second wife, lived until her death in 1955. This memorial, which is now a museum, houses much of London's South Sea collection, his desk, writing and dictating equipment, and scores of mementos.

The return trip down the hill from the park will take you to the right at the bottom of the hill (in Glen Ellen) on Arnold Drive. Arnold Drive passes through the beautiful grounds of the State Mental Hospital, past the Hanna Center for Boys and finally to the little community of El Verano which is only two miles from the center of Sonoma. You should turn left from Arnold Drive at the sign pointing to El Verano.

Two other historical highlights are within easy reach of the cyclist in Sonoma. One is a visit to the Sonoma State Historical Park including the Vallejo home and the Sonoma Mission and barracks, which are on the north side of the square. An excellent delicatessen is located on this side of the square also. Here you may wish to gather French bread, cheeses and meats for a thoroughly enjoyable picnic at another fascinating point of interest — the Buena Vista Winery. The Buena Vista is the parent of all of California's premium wineries. The vineyards here were founded in 1832 by Hungarian-born Count Agoston Haraszthy who became the "Father of California Viticulture." Haraszthy imported thousands of cuttings from the finest vineyards in France, Germany, Italy and Hungary. The winery is located in a beautiful grove of giant eucalyptus trees among which are two large, old vine-covered stone buildings housing the wine cellar and tasting room and the crushing room. Picnic tables around a pleasant, bubbling fountain are located in front of one of the stone buildings. To get to the Buena Vista Winery take East Napa Street east to Old Winery Road, just across the railroad tracks about a mile from the town square. Go left or north on Old Winery Road about a 0.3 mile to the winery.

*"House of The Happy Walls"*

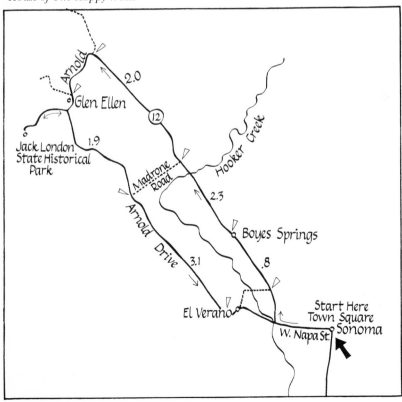

# 20 BICYCLING IN SEBASTOPOL? ?

**General location: North Bay Counties - Santa Rosa**
**Distance: 24 miles round trip**
**Riding time: 2 - 3 hours**
**Road/Traffic conditions: Very good/Light - Moderate**
**Facilities: Sebastopol, Valley Ford**
**Ride Rating: ★★**

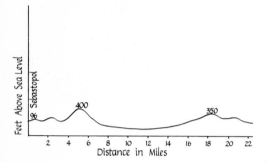

California's answer to the Russian city of Sevastopol is located in Sonoma County northeast of Petaluma at the junction of State Highways 116 and 12. To reach Sebastopol take either Highway 12 or 116 west from U.S. 101 or go east on these same roads from the coast.

Sebastopol is located in the same kind of rolling, oak-studded hills characteristic of many areas in the North Bay counties. The town itself is small and quiet and is in the center of an agricultural and dairying region. The ride is in a very rural setting and goes up, down and through truly beautiful countryside.

Sebastopol derived its curious name from a fight which took place between two men in 1855. The story is that one man barricaded himself inside Dougherty's store in the community to gain protection against his attacker. Onlookers dubbed the store "Sebastopol" in reference to the Crimean War siege which was taking place at that time. The name of the store stuck, and as the town grew this name was adopted.

The Sebastopol area is also well-known for its apples, and as you ride this trip you will pass by many apple orchards. The greatest portion of apples grown here are of the Gravenstein variety. They are large, yellow apples striped with red and are most abundant in the area called Gold Ridge, which is located between Sebastopol and Bloomfield. As you ride through these apple orchards and grazing fields on the country backroads of Sebastopol you will probably hear the cowbells, the meadowlark's trill and bullfrogs chorusing in roadside marshes. Along the way, at about the half-way point, you'll pass through Valley Ford and Bloomfield, two very small, very quiet, little villages. If you were speeding along in an automobile and blinked at the wrong moment, you'd probably miss some of the unique sights, sounds, and smells of these little communities.

After leaving Bloomfield you'll be confronted with a rather long, but not too steep hill climbing to the top of Gold Ridge. Once to the top, the road descends back to the Gravenstein Highway (State 116) and downtown Sebastopol.

64

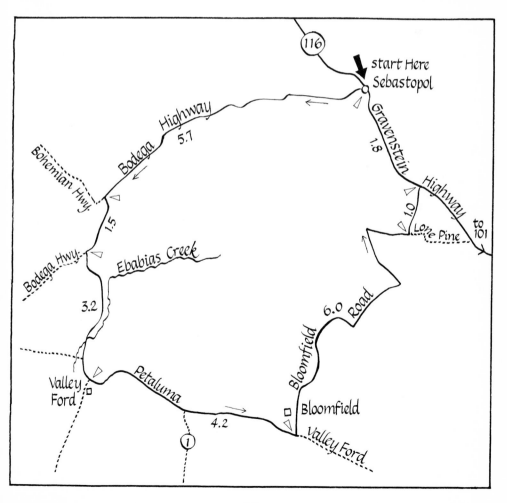

116

start Here
Sebastopol

Bodega Highway 5.7

Bohemian Hwy.

Gravenstein Highway
1.8

1.0
Lone Pine

to 101

Bodega Hwy. 1.5

Ebabias Creek

3.2

Bloomfield Road 6.0

Valley Ford

Petaluma

4.2

1

Bloomfield

Valley Ford

# 21 ELEPHANT ROCKS

**General location: Tomales, north of Point Reyes**
**Distance: 16.3 miles round trip**
**Riding time: 2 - 3½ hours**
**Road/Traffic conditions: Very good/Light**
**Facilities: Tomales, Valley Ford**
**Ride rating: * ***

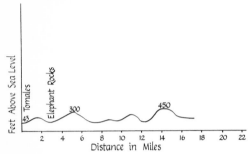

The large Elephant Rocks near Tomales Bay are one of thé main attractions on this trip. They resemble hulking grey elephants standing face to face and are ideal climbing rocks. If you bring a picnic lunch, stop here and enjoy the beautiful view of Dillon Beach and Bodega Bay to the west and explore the many nooks, crannies and caves in and around the Elephant Rocks.

The town of Tomales, only 4.5 miles from Bodega Bay is the starting point of this tour to Valley Ford and back. Tomales is west of Petaluma and the town itself is just north of the junction of Coast Highway 1 and Tomales-Petaluma Road. Please note that Tomales-Petaluma Road undergoes an interesting road name change metamorphosis from Tomales to Petaluma. Tomales-Petaluma Road becomes Petaluma-Valley Ford Road which finally becomes Bodega Avenue near Petaluma. By taking Coast Highway 1 north from Mill Valley and past Pt. Reyes Station you can also reach the town of Tomales at the northernmost end of Tomales Bay.

Although this ride is relatively short in distance, it has several significant hills. The land is rather barren with only occasional trees, mounds of rock or farm buildings to break the smooth hills. You will cross both the Estero de San Juan Antonio and the Estero Americano on Valley Ford - Franklin School Road (another instance of name change). Esteros are brackish inland waterways, which, in this case, lead out to Bodega Bay. The road is quite narrow on this trip but it is in good condition and is lightly traveled by motorized vehicles.

The town of Tomales is neat and quaint looking and is located on the western side of Marin County in countryside known for its butter, cheese and milk. The town's first house was built in 1850 by a man who operated a schooner between Tomales and San Francisco, and who, four years later, built the first trading post in Tomales. The Spanish word Tomales is believed to have evolved from the Coast Miwok Indian word "Tamal", meaning bay.

At some points on this trip you will be able to view Bodega Bay, which is now a shallow, sand-choked, mud-rimmed inlet and therefore not valuable commercially as a shipping center. The bay was named after Lieutenant Juan Francisco de la Bodega y Cuadra who anchored his schooner, the Sonora, off Bodega Head in 1775. The Russians were also active in the area. They planted wheat on the land bordering the bay, erected warehouses, trapped thousands of sea otters and in 1811, founded two settlements on Bodega Bay. The first Americans to settle in the Bodega Bay vicinity were three sailors who were given land grants on the condition that they would check the Russian incursion into the territory. The area around Bodega in the 1860's bustled with activity. Harbors were crowded with sailing ships, freight and passenger boats. The economic mainstay of the area was a variety of potato known as the Bodega Red.

Valley Ford, with its population of 125 persons, and its elevation of 53 feet above sea level, lies at the head of the Estero Americano (American Creek) which empties into Bodega Bay. It was named for the "valley ford" where an old Indian and Spanish trail crossed the Estero. Like Tomales, Valley Ford is a dairy town.

*Elephant Rocks*

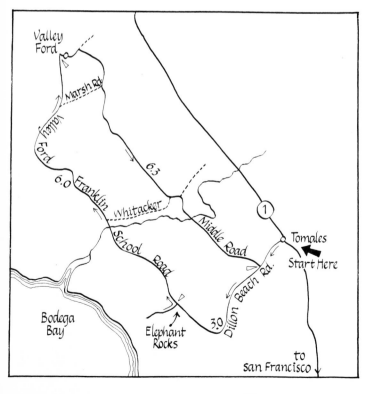

Valley Ford

Marsh Rd.

Valley Ford

6.3

6.0 Franklin

Whitacker

School Road

Middle Road

1

Tomales

Start Here

Dillon Beach Rd.

3.0

Bodega Bay

Elephant Rocks

to san Francisco

# 22 RUSSIAN RIVER

**General location: Santa Rosa - Sonoma County**
**Distance: 19 miles round trip**
**Riding time: 1½ - 2½ hours**
**Road/Traffic conditions: Very good — wide**
**shoulder most of way/Moderate-Heavy (de-**
**pending on season)**
**Facilities: Rio Nido, Guerneville**
**Ride rating: ** **

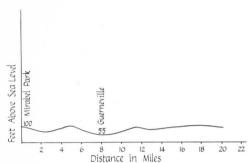

The starting point for your ride down the Russian River is located at Mirabel Park at the junction of River Road and Mirabel Road. River Road goes west from U.S. 101 at Fulton, which is just north of Santa Rosa. River Road does not actually meet the Russian River until the Mirabel Park junction. An alternate route to reach Mirabel Park from the south is to take California 116 (the Gravenstein Highway) north from Cotati, which is on U.S. 101. Then, when you reach Forestville, take Mirabel Road north to Mirabel Park. There is adequate parking at the Mirabel - River Road junction area.

Bicycling in the relatively flat Russian River country always provides the cyclist with a day of fun, fresh air and matchless scenery. The Russian River region from Mirabel Park to Guerneville has been a popular resort area since the days of early San Francisco, and for good reason. Boating or canoeing, fishing, camping, picnicking and, of course, bicycling are recreational activities which many people in northern California find enjoyable. Although most of these diversions are seasonal, cycling isn't. Given reasonably good weather, cyclists can enjoy the Russian River any time of year.

Guerneville is a small trade center known especially for its apple growing. Although it is relatively quiet in the winter, its summer population expands to about ten times its winter size. Guerneville is fishing headquarters for steelhead and salmon during winter months and small mouth bass during the summer.

The Korbel Champagne Cellars between Rio Nido and the Hacienda on the River Road is well worth visiting. This champagne producing facility, surrounded by vineyard-covered rolling hills, uses several old world methods to make their product more natural.

Mirabel Park has an elevation of 100 feet and Guerneville only 55 feet, but Mt. Jackson and Black Mountain on the north side of the Russian River rise to altitudes of 1655 and 1450 feet respectively. Although in the middle of some fairly steep and mountainous country, the River Road follows the Russian River very closely all the way to Guerneville and makes for a very gradual and pleasant bicycle journey.

*Russian River*

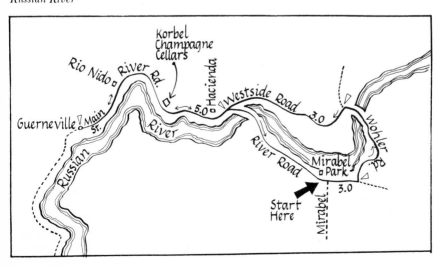

# 23 CHEESE FACTORY — PETALUMA

**General location:** North Bay — Petaluma
**Distance:** 22 miles round trip
**Riding time:** 2 - 3½ hours
**Road/Traffic conditions:** Good; bumpy, narrow shoulders in places/Moderate
**Facilities:** Cheese, sandwiches, drinks at cheese factory; Petaluma
**Ride rating:** **

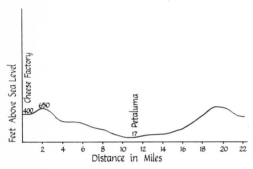

The Marin French Cheese Company, which is a real cheese production plant, is located just west of Novato Boulevard on Petaluma (Red Hill) Road. To reach the old cheese factory, take either South Novato Boulevard to Petaluma Road or D Street from Petaluma west to the cheese factory. D Street becomes Red Hill or Petaluma Road.

This ride is situated in some very pretty farm country north of San Francisco and is characterized by rolling, live oak-studded hills and grazing dairy cattle. During late winter and early spring the hills look like rounded mounds of velvet with occasional outcroppings of rugged rocks. In the summer green turns to golden brown but the countryside retains its tranquil beauty. This ride is, for the most part, an enjoyable downward trip to Petaluma, but alas, for the cyclist, what goes down must come up. And this is just what will be facing you as you return to the cheese factory via Western and Chileno Valley Roads. On the road to Petaluma you'll encounter only one relatively short hill before descending on Red Hill Road to Petaluma. When you reach Petaluma go left on 4th (at the small city park) to Western Avenue which is only a couple blocks over. Then turn left again on Western for the return trip. Watch for the junction where Western jogs sharply to the left becoming Chileno Valley Road, while Spring Hill Road goes straight. If you go straight you may end up at Two Rock, which is exactly nowhere. Once on Chileno Valley Road you will experience a tough climb of about a mile to the top of a rather substantial hill. You may decide that discretion is the better part of valor and choose to walk up a portion of this grade. Once to the top, however, the remainder of your journey should be relatively level. On the other side of the hill, at the bottom, turn sharply to the left.

The old cheese factory, where you will begin the trip, has been making cheese since the mid 1800's. An interesting and informative tour is provided through the factory. "Factory" is a word that one probably shouldn't think of in the traditional sense when referring to this small, efficient but definitely family operated business. The cheese making and aging rooms are kept immaculate in the smelly underground production area and the finished products attest to the care and quality of the cheese-making process. The cheese tasting room may have "seconds" for sale as well as the regularly packaged cheeses, which are equal in quality but are slightly below acceptable weight. If you're interested in buying some ROUGE ET NOIR cheese, after tasting, you may be able to save a few cents. The cheese factory also has pleasant picnic facilities located in front of the main building, which you may wish to take advantage of either before or after the ride.

The town name of Petaluma is an Indian word meaning "beautiful view". Petaluma was first settled in 1833 and became an active commercial center in 1878 largely due to the efforts of one man — a young Canadian named Lyman Ryce. He introduced Petaluma and the world to large scale poultry raising with his artificial incubators and brooders and his hearty leghorn variety of chicken.

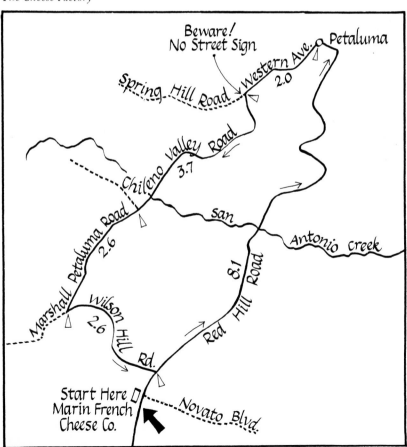

*The Cheese Factory*

Beware!
No Street Sign

Petaluma

Spring Hill Road

Western Ave.
2.0

Chileno Valley Road
3.7

Marshall Petaluma Road
2.6

San

Antonio Creek

Red Hill Road
8.1

Wilson Hill Rd.
2.6

Start Here
Marin French
Cheese Co.

Novato Blvd.

# 24   CLEAR LAKE — KELSEYVILLE

**General location: North Bay Counties - Clear Lake**
**Distance: 12 miles round trip**
**Riding time: 45 min. - 1½ hours**
**Road/Traffic conditions: Excellent/Light Moderate**
**Facilities: Kelseyville**
**Ride rating: \***

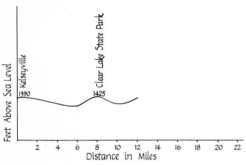

Clear Lake, the largest freshwater lake within the state, is about 28 miles long and up to 9 miles wide. The lake is rather shallow in most places and really is more of a clouded greenish hue rather than clear. Both Clear Lake and Kelseyville, the starting point of this trip, are located in Lake County on State Highway 29. Kelseyville can be reached from the west by taking State Highway 175 from the town of Hopland on U.S. 101; from the south, by taking either State Highway 175 or 29 north from Middletown; from the east take State Highways 20 and 53 to Highway 29 at Lower Lake; and from the north follow State Highway 20 south from U.S. 101 above Ukiah.

The Kelseyville cycling trip, which goes through pear orchards, Clear Lake State Park and along a small portion of the lake front is, for the most part, quite level. The only exception is a short, steep hill in Clear Lake State Park. Views of the surrounding countryside from Soda Bay Road and from atop the hill in the State Park offer the cyclist a superb panorama of one of California's loveliest mountain and lake regions, resembling sections in the highlands of Scotland. The most noticeable topographic feature of the area is Mt. Konocti to the south, rising to an elevation of 4200 feet.

Kelseyville, (population 200) a sleepy little village in the off-season and a bustling resort town during the summer, is called "Peartown" for the thick groves of pear orchards surrounding it. Kelseyville was first settled in the early 1800's by Antonio and Salvador Vallejo who built a log cabin in the Kelseyville vicinity. In 1847 their land was sold to Benjamin Kelsey, Charles Stone and others. When Kelsey and Stone had local Pomo Indians build them a home, they earned the enmity of their laborers by their unkindness, and in revenge the Indians killed them both in 1849.

Outside of Kelseyville you will pass through rows and rows of pear trees on some of the lightly-traveled back roads of Kelseyville before coming to Kelseyville  Soda Bay Road, where you will turn left toward Clear Lake State Park. Soda Bay Road is flat and descends gradually toward the Park and Clear Lake.

Turn left at the entrance to Clear Lake State Park and proceed past the entry gate and the first campground toward the lake. Entry fees are not charged to cyclists just riding through the park and not using the camping or picnicking facilities. This 560-acre State Park includes some 11,200 feet of beach and lake frontage. The park itself is beautifully wooded with such shrubs and trees as western redbud, · manzanita, mountain mahogany, digger pine, blue oak and valley oak. A boat ramp and swimming beaches are available in the park near the 28-unit picnic area and Bayview Campground. The area where the park is now located was once occupied by the peaceful Pomo Indians, who were famous for their basket weaving. An Indian site in the park where sweat and other ceremonial houses were located is being restored. The Pomo used what is now the park's Moki beach for canoe landings. When white men began to settle the area about 1840 the Indians were moved from their favorite lands to reservations and their living conditions and traditional way of life changed.

Some of the birds which can be seen in the park are ducks, coots, gulls, pelicans and valley quail. All of these birds use the park's protected land as a refuge. Fishermen try their luck on the lake's crappie, catfish, black bass and bluegill, and hikers or cyclists in the park are likely to see some of the many black-tailed deer, or black-tailed hare, brush rabbit, ground squirrel or chipmunk.

The return trip to Kelseyville from the state park will take you up the hill and through the upper Bayview Campground, past the locked gate at the top of the hill, which is closed to auto traffic, and then down the back side of the hill to Soda Bay Road. Go right at Soda Bay Road and follow this pleasant route back to downtown Kelseyville.

*Looking toward Mt. Konocti*

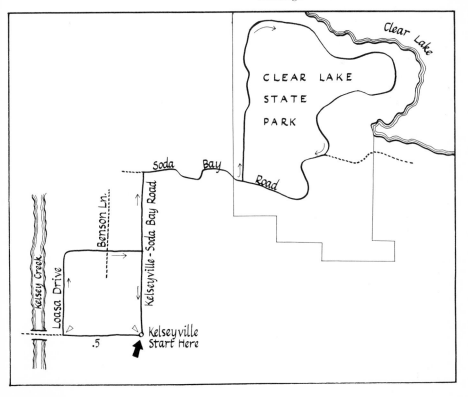

# 25 CLEAR LAKE — 'ROUND MT. KONOCHTI

**General location: North Bay Counties; Clear Lake**
**Distance: 22 miles round trip**
**Riding time: 2 - 3 hours**
**Road/Traffic conditions: Fair - Good/Moderate - Heavy**
**Facilities: Kelseyville, Soda Bay**
**Ride rating: ★★**

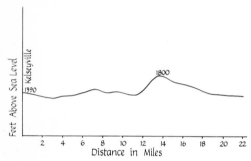

Riding around lofty Mt. Konochti (4200′) is the goal of this scenic loop starting in the little village of Kelseyville. Kelseyville is located just to the west of Clear Lake on State Highway 29 in Lake County. To get there take State Highway 175 east from Hopland on 101 or either State 175 or 29 north from Middletown if you are coming from Calistoga. From the east, Clear Lake can be reached by Highways 20 and 53 to Highway 29 at Lower Lake; and from the north, take highway 20 south from U.S. 101 just above Ukiah.

The beginning of this loop around Mt. Konochti starts in the town of Kelseyville, which has been called "Pear-town" by its boosters. Although Kelseyville is only a short way from Clear Lake,

the lake is not visible from the town because of intervening Mt. Konochti and the heavily wooded land near the lake itself. This trip is characterized by short rolling hills as the Soda Bay Road skirts Clear Lake. Superb views of the lake and surrounding area are offered from several vantage points on the trip. There are several hills on this tour, the most substantial of which is located just south of Mt. Konochti. This hill has an elevation gain of 500 feet and will provide a genuine challenge to most cyclists. After crossing the summit of this hill and moving out of the view of Clear Lake toward the west side of Mt. Konochti, the countryside becomes much more pastoral, in no way resembling the resort-like lakeside area.

You will ride through this rolling, wooded farmland all the way back to Kelseyville.

The most noticeable feature on this loop besides the lake is, of course, Mt. Konochti. This impressive mountain peak, often shrouded in clouds, is steeped in local Pomo Indian tradition. The Pomo dwelt on the shores around the lake as well as on its islands, some of which are clearly visible from many points on this ride. They ferried across and around the lake on tule balsas (rafts) and originated the legend about Mt. Konochti. The story the Indians told was how mighty Chief Konochti became angry when his enemy, Chief Kahbel asked for his daughter Lupiyomi in marriage. His rage forced him into battle with Kahbel at the Narrows — where a long tongue of land almost cuts the lake in two. Across the water the two chiefs hurled huge boulders at each other which strew the mountainside until Kahbel lay dead and Konochti, dying, fell back to form Mt. Konochti (4200′) which towers between the two arms of the lake east of the Narrows.

Although the Pomo were once masters of the lake, their memory and lore are all that remain. Many of the Indians were slaughtered across the lake at Nice just before the "Treaty of Peace and Friendship" in 1851. In this treaty the Indians agreed to give up their lands for a gift of 10 head of cattle, 3 sacks of bread and sundry clothing.

*Soda Bay Road*

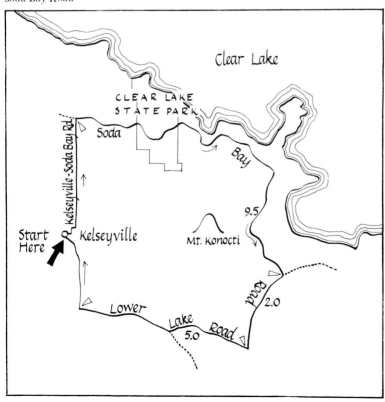

Clear Lake

CLEAR LAKE
STATE PARK

Kelseyville-Soda Bay Rd.

Soda

Bay

9.5

Start
Here

Kelseyville

Mt. Konocti

Road

2.0

Lower

Lake    Road

5.0

# 26 RUSSIAN GULCH RIDE — MENDOCINO

**General location: Mendocino**
**Distance: 4.5 miles up and back**
**Riding time: ½ - ¾ hour**
**Road/Traffic conditions: Excellent/Light**
**Facilities: Picnicking in Russian Gulch State Park**
**Ride rating: ***

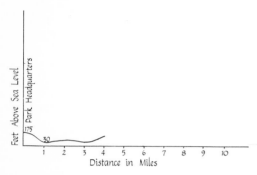

Russian Gulch State Park is located on California's rugged northern coastline 10 miles south of Ft. Bragg and 2.5 miles north of Mendocino. This part of the coast is most easily reached by taking State Highway 128 west from Cloverdale or Highway 20 west from Willits.

This ride is very short, very enjoyable and breathtakingly beautiful. It starts at the ranger station south of the entrance to the park and winds down under the coast Highway bridge, which stands high above Russian Gulch. Spectacular views of the surf crashing on the headland rocks jutting out into the sea, the beach area

and the beautiful bridge are visible from the vicinity of the ranger station. The ride up shaded Russian Gulch Canyon is delightfully cool and the paved, lightly-traveled pathway parallels Russian Gulch Creek all of the way. Along the route you'll pass a couple of gushing waterfalls (more active in early season) and will enjoy the serenity of the forest and the absence of any motorized vehicles.

Russian Gulch State Park is open for camping from April through October but the bike trail up Russian Gulch is accessible to cyclists any time of year. The Park extends inland about 3 miles from the ranger station and most of this distance is covered by the Russian Gulch Scenic Road which you'll follow. Russian Gulch Falls (52 feet high) may be seen by taking a foot trail from the end of the Scenic Road. This Falls Loop Trail is 3.5 miles long and passes through some dense stands of second-growth coast redwoods which fill the canyon. Also found in the park are Douglas fir, hemlock, tanoak and California laurel.

Out on the headland (the rocky promontory jutting out into the ocean) a deep sea-cut tunnel some 200 feet long exists. This tunnel has collapsed to form a hole 100 feet across and 60 feet deep and offers a spectacular sight to park visitors. You can cycle out to the parking area on the headland, which is only about one-fourth mile west of the ranger station. Waves can be seen coming through the tunnel but the bowl is too broad and open to qualify it as a "blow hole," although several such blowholes may be seen along the Mendocino coast.

Raccoons, rabbits, chipmunks and deer are the animals seen most frequently although skunks, bobcats and foxes also make their homes in the area. Birdlife is plentiful. There are many of the common Stellar jays and quail, band-tailed pigeons, hawks, and ravens.

Another attraction in the park is the Pygmy Forest which can be reached from the north trail (a foot trail north of the Scenic Road). The forest is in the northeastern portion of the park and consists of dwarfed Mendocino Cypress trees which have grown slowly in the highly acidic, almost white "podsoils" found there.

A helpful suggestion in cycling in the Mendocino area is to avoid riding on Coast Highway 1 if at all possible. Although this road is not as narrow from Little River to Ft. Bragg as it is along other places of the coast, the roadway almost always has no shoulder on which to ride, and is heavily and speedily traveled by motorized vehicles. If you want to do some more cycling, take some colorful side trips in the little seaside villages of Mendocino, Caspar and Little River where great little shops, restaurants and antique stores abound. Bikes are for rent at the Soup Kitchen in Mendocino, in case you want to take a spin around the town and didn't bring your bike along. A 5.0 mile up and back "safe" cycling route is also available in Van Damme State Park south of Mendocino at Little River. And for the more rugged, consider the rather hilly circle ride from Little River toward Comptche on the Little River Comptche Road and Comptche Ukiah Road (13 miles). Another great ride starting in Ft. Bragg is documented in trip 27.

*Bridge over Russian Gulch*

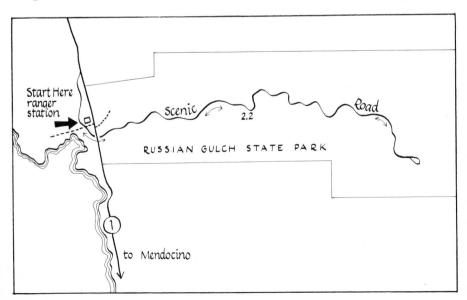

# 27 FT. BRAGG LOGGING ROAD RAMBLE

**General location:** Ft. Bragg - Mendocino
**Distance:** 15 miles round trip
**Riding time:** 1½ - 2½ hours
**Road/Traffic conditions:** Excellent/Light
**Facilities:** Ft. Bragg; picnicking along the beach or on Ten Mile River
**Ride rating:** **

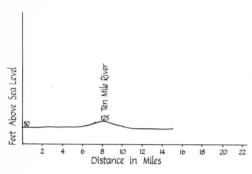

*Beach near logging road*

The starting point for this ride can be reached by going north through Ft. Bragg on Coast Highway 1 to the northern part of town. There, just past the prominent Baxman Gravel pit is a left hand turnoff where several huge yellow lumber trucks are usually parked. Start here.

Although this trip offers beautiful scenery, superb road and traffic conditions and is super flat, it is on private property and is therefore a conditional ride. First, those large yellow lumber trucks run on this road during the week (Monday through Friday) making it impossible to ride on those days. Second, if the large red gate at the west end of the lot is in the up position on weekends, it may mean that trucks are operating and the road is impassable. Third, there are usually some men at the truck depot who you should ask for permission to ride on the road before you start. If all of these conditions are go, this is a fantastic bicycle ride along the ocean, through MacKerricher State Park north of Ft. Bragg and, finally, up Tenmile Road to the bridge across Tenmile River. The right of way on the road you'll be following is owned by Boise Cascade and the

giant trucks you will see at the trip start bring huge redwood trees down from the hills to be milled in Ft. Bragg.

You will go north on this ride parallel to the ocean for most of the way. Large, small and unusually shaped pieces of driftwood line the sandy beaches as you proceed along the route to Tenmile River. If you brought a picnic lunch, you may want to park your bike alongside a sand dune and relax on the beach. At the northern end of the ride where the road turns east up Tenmile River, the cool, blustery ocean breezes usually calm and the inland temperatures begin to climb. Tenmile River is clear and sparkling and looks extremely inviting on hot days. Tenmile Road becomes dirt and gravel about .8 mile from the bridge and, therefore, it is not desirable to continue once the heavy, wood-planked bridge is reached.

Ft. Bragg, the starting point for this trip, is primarily a lumbering center, but also markets poultry, dairy products, and seafood. The town was established in 1857 by Lt. Horatio Gibson as a military post. It was named after General Braxton Bragg of Mexican War fame. The town is settled today mainly by people of Finnish and Swedish descent.

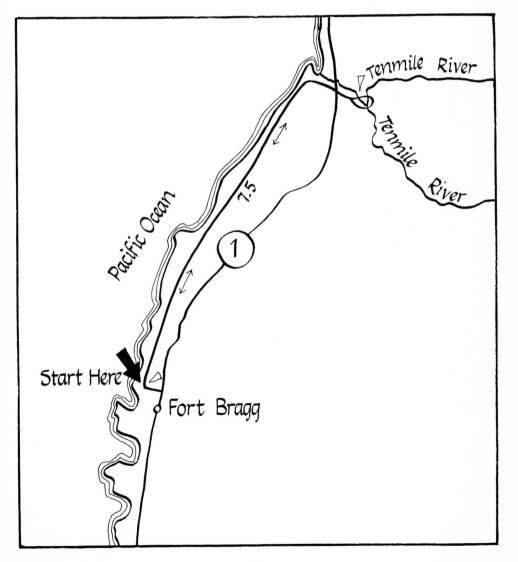

Tenmile River

Tenmile River

Pacific Ocean

7.5

①

Start Here

Fort Bragg

# 28 BOULDER CREEK — BIG BASIN REDWOODS LOOP

**General location: Boulder Creek (near Santa Cruz)**
**Distance: 26 miles round trip**
**Riding time: 3 - 4 hours**
**Road/Traffic conditions: Good; narrow/Moderate - heavy**
**Facilities: Boulder Creek; restrooms, water, small store (summers only) in Big Basin Redwoods State Park**
**Ride rating: * * ***

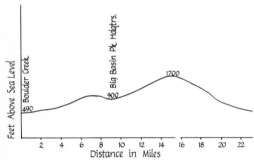

Boulder Creek, originally a redwood lumber camp but now a summer resort center, is the starting point for this scenic tour. Boulder Creek is located on State Highway 9 between Saratoga and Santa Cruz. It is approximately 21 miles from Saratoga and 14 miles from Santa Cruz.

This loop will take you through some rather steep, heavily-wooded, mountainous country, and is not recommended for beginning cyclists. To tackle the full loop you should be in good condition and should have a moderate amount of riding experience.

State Highway 236 is the route you should take out of Boulder Creek toward Big Basin Redwoods State Park. En route to the giant redwoods you will gradually climb upwards passing many resort homes, the Rainbow Trout Park, and the Boulder Creek Golf Course. Near Sunnyside Lodge you will reach the crest of the first major grade out of Boulder Creek and will begin a 2.7 mile downhill coast into the state park. This downgrade will take you through some spectacular towering Redwoods as you come nearer to Big Basin Park Headquarters.

Big Basin Redwoods State Park was established in 1902 and is the oldest park now in the California park system. In 1769 it is believed that the party of Gaspar de Portola, an early Spanish explorer, passed just to the west of the park along the coast. The park comprises about 12,000 acres of forested land, 35 miles of hiking trails and an interesting variety of plants and animals. The most magnificent of the plant life, of course, are the giant coast redwood trees. Some of the tallest and oldest redwoods are found here. The tree named "Father of the Forest", near park headquarters is some 2000 years old. Nearby "Mother of the Forest" is 329 feet high, the tallest in the park, and the "Santa Clara Tree" has a giant diameter of nearly 17 feet.

Some of the animals to be found in the park include Columbian black-tailed deer, commonly seen adjacent to the ranger headquarters building, raccoons, Merriam chipmunks, the large blue Stellars jay and the Oregon junco, a small bird with a black head and cape. Animals which exist in the park but are seen less often include opposum, fox, coyote, weasel and bobcat. During the summer season concessionaires operate a restaurant, snack bar, gift shop and auto service station.

Highway 236 going north or up from the headquarters building provides the cyclist with a rather rigorous and challenging climb. Nauseously termed "car sick alley" by many motorists, this 8.4 mile stretch of State 236 is winding and narrow (barely enough room for two cars to pass in places.) From many points on this road you will be able to view the Pacific Ocean and much of the thickly-wooded, green expanse of the park.

After reaching Highway 9 at Waterman Gap (1267') you will find an almost entirely downhill grade for the 7.5 mile return trip to Boulder Creek. Both before and after Waterman Gap you should take special care when riding in the intermittent sun and shade on this wooded road. The sun-shade phenomenon especially as you move rapidly down hill, can obscure the road from your vision. It also decreases your visability as a cyclist to automobiles, since drivers are subject to the same conditions.

*Big Basin Redwoods State Park*

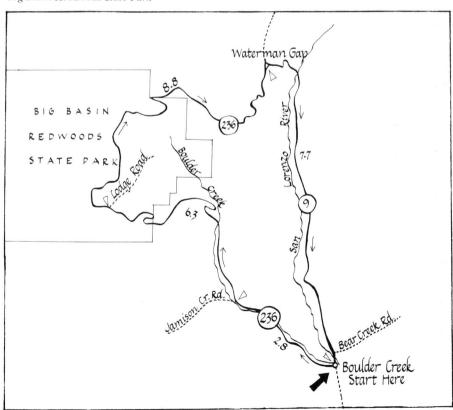

Waterman Gap

BIG BASIN
REDWOODS
STATE PARK

8.8

236

7.7

Lodge Road

Boulder Creek

9

San Lorenzo River

6.3

Jamison Cr. Rd.

236

Bear Creek Rd.

2.8

Boulder Creek
Start Here

# 29 CHESBRO AND UVAS RESERVOIR CIRCLE TOUR

**General location: Morgan Hill - Gilroy (south of San Jose)**
**Distance: 16.7 miles round trip**
**Riding time: 1½ - 2½ hours**
**Road/Traffic conditions: Very good/Moderate**
**Facilities: Trip start**
**Ride rating: * ***

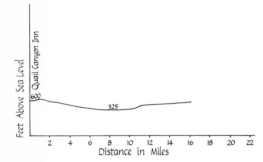

This mostly flat reservoir loop ride south of San Jose is a favorite of many South Bay residents. To reach its starting point, the Quail Canyon Inn, take U.S. 101 south toward Morgan Hill and Gilroy. Just before reaching the Morgan Hill city limits sign, turn west on Tilton Avenue. Refer to the map for the turns you will have to negotiate before reaching the Quail Canyon Inn on Chesbro Reservoir.

The roads on this trip, although narrow in some places, wind lazily through the farming and orchard land surrounding Chesbro and Uvas Reservoirs. Patches of live oak clustered on the nearby hills are easily visible as well as on the more thickly wooded, higher hills to the west. Although hills surround the ride route, there are few of any consequence to climb on this tour. Some of the prettiest and most impressive scenery on this trip can be found along Llagas Creek in Paradise Valley. Here, the bubbling creek and the beautiful orchards of prunes and walnuts are nestled between two rows of low hills. Since this part of the trip is near the end of the ride, a rest and relaxation stop may be in order.

Although much of the land along the Chesbro-Uvas cycle route is filled with small farms and fruit or nut orchards today, the view 80 years ago was one of unbroken miles of grain and hay. The entire area around Morgan Hill, some 10,000 acres, was part of a massive estate owned by Daniel Murphy. He was the son of Martin Murphy, patriarch of a large Irish family which came overland to California in 1844. In the 1870's Daniel hired Hiram Morgan Hill, his brother-in-law, to manage his estate. The land included the general area covered on this tour as well as large portions of three Mexican land grants. One of them, Las Uvas (The Grapes), undoubtedly influenced the naming of Uvas Reservoir. During summer months, when the reservoirs have adequate water, this area is popular for boating, water skiing, and fishing. Although the water may look very inviting on a hot summer day, please observe the "No Swimming" signs posted at each reservoir.

*Uvas Reservoir Area*

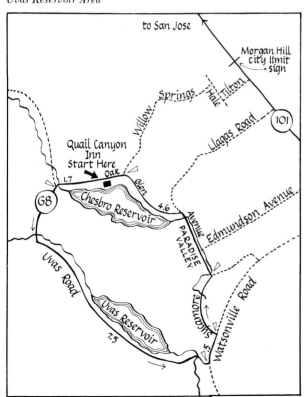

# 30 MOUNT MADONNA HILL CLIMBERS' DELIGHT

**General location: Morgan Hill - Gilroy (south of San Jose)**
**Distance: 38.3 miles round trip**
**Riding time: 3 - 4½ hours**
**Road/Traffic conditions: Good/Moderate - heavy**
**Facilities: Trip start, atop Hecker Pass, picnicking Mount Madonna County Park**
**Ride rating: \* \* \***

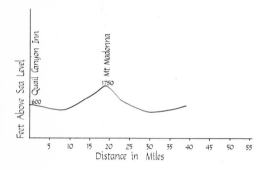

If you're a hill-climbing, longer distance buff and are searching for something a bit more challenging, you'll thoroughly enjoy this ride. Like trip 29, this trip begins at the Quail Canyon Inn west of Morgan Hill. To reach this starting point, take U.S. 101 south toward Gilroy and turn right (west) just before reaching the Morgan Hill city limit sign. Proceed west on Tilton Avenue and wind your way (please refer to map) to Chesbro Reservoir.

This ride is relatively flat, except, of course, the 5.1 mile climb up Mount Madonna. You will first pass many of the small farms and orchards in the rolling hills along Chesbro and Uvas Reservoirs. Beyond the sprawling D'Arrigo Brothers Cactus Pear Ranch on State Highway 152, the countryside becomes more wooded and the road steeper.

Most of the land on this tour was owned by early California settler Daniel Murphy who was the son of Martin Murphy, one of California's first settlers who came west in 1849. Daniel Murphy accumulated a large estate during his lifetime and part of it, some 10,000 acres, was located in the general area of this ride. Although much of the land today is a patchwork of small farms and orchards, the view in the late 1800's was one of unbroken miles of grain and hay.

The Hecker Pass Highway, or State Highway 152, was named after Henry Hecker (1862-1948) who had always dreamed and worked for a final link in the Yosemite-to-the-Sea highway. As you climb this road, try to visualize it as it once was — a deeply rutted, rough dirt trail originally used as a redwood lumber mill logging road. This route is now known and appreciated as one of the area's prettiest drives, offering a splendid view of the Santa Clara Valley and the ocean from atop Hecker Pass (1309'). The state now includes the route in its scenic highway system.

If you are interested in doing a bit of wine tasting on this tour, two small family-owned wineries and tasting rooms exist along Watsonville Road (68) and State 152. First, on Watsonville Road is the Bonesia Winery and Tasting Room (open 8 a.m. to 6 p.m. daily). On State 152 (Hecker Pass Road), across the road from the Cactus Pear Ranch, is the Fortino Brothers Winery and Tasting Room (open 8 a.m. to 5 p.m.). Above the Hecker Pass Road summit around lofty Mount Madonna (1897') is Mount Madonna County Park. In the park are hiking and horseback riding trails, picnicking and camping facilities, and a fishing lake for children. Near the central picnic grounds in the park is a group of white Fallow deer, originally from the Mediterranean area. They are small in stature and are interesting to observe in their enclosed area.

*White Fallow Deer*

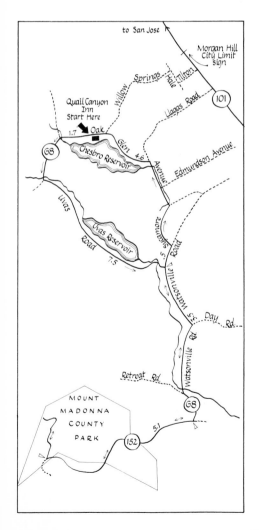

# 31 NATURAL BRIDGES — U.C. SANTA CRUZ

**General location: Santa Cruz**
**Distance: 10 miles round trip**
**Riding time: 1 - 2 hours**
**Road/Traffic conditions: Good/Moderate**
**Facilities: Picnicking at Natural Bridges; Santa Cruz**
**Ride rating: ***

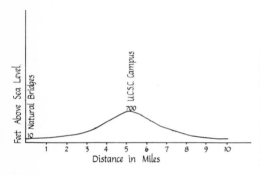

A short and very enjoyable ride which can be coupled with a day at the beach is waiting for you at Natural Bridges State Beach in Santa Cruz. To reach Natural Bridges on the north side of Santa Cruz take either State Highway 1 north toward Half Moon Bay from State Highway 17 or if you're coming south on State Highway 1, look for the Natural Bridges State Beach sign on the northern outskirts of Santa Cruz.

Natural Bridges State Beach is an excellent starting place for the trip and is also a good picnicking and beaching spot. The naturally eroded sandstone arches or bridges make this state beach unique and the tide pools here are some of the best and most interesting on the coast.

The monarch butterfly makes his home in great numbers at Natural Bridges State Beach from late fall through early spring. Thousands of these interesting and beautiful creatures migrate each year to a sheltered grove of red-gum (Eucalyptus rostarata) just south of the entry gate to the state beach. Some of the monarchs come from as far away as northern Canada. When temperatures are cool, the monarchs are noted for clustering in large masses on the trees. To the casual observer they might appear to be dead leaves on a limb. As the temperatures rise, however, the butterflies spread their wings and the trees seem to burst into bloom.

The University of California Santa Cruz campus, which you'll ride through, begins just after you turn from Escalona Drive onto Bay Drive. Bay Drive ascends to the top of a hill where most of the dormitory, classroom and administrative buildings may be found. U.C. Santa Cruz was opened in 1965 on the former Cowell Ranch northwest of Santa Cruz. The university is located on 2000 acres of partly forested land overlooking the city and Monterey Bay. The view of the city of Santa Cruz, Monterey Bay and the beaches from Glen Coolidge Drive is outstanding. The old buildings on Bay Drive on the campus probably were part of the Cowell Ranch and have been preserved intact. The student and administration buildings on the upper campus are attractive. They are quite modernistic in design and are nestled in groups on the heavily-forested campus.

The return trip from the campus hilltop is a very enjoyable downhill jaunt which should make all your uphill efforts seem worthwhile.

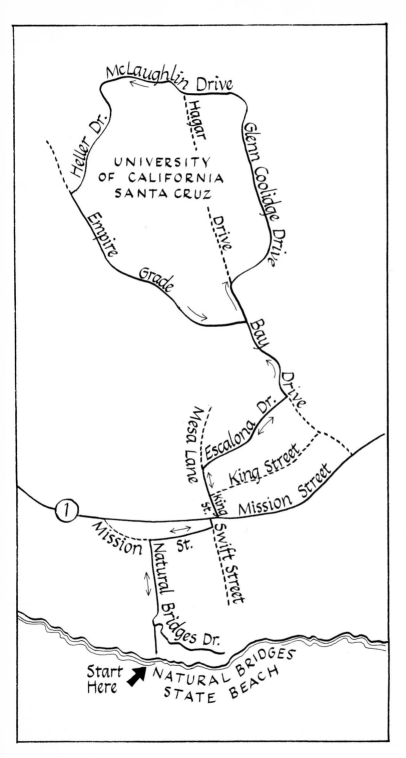

McLaughlin Drive

Heller Dr.

Hagar

Glenn Coolidge Drive

UNIVERSITY
OF CALIFORNIA
SANTA CRUZ

Empire

Drive

Grade

Bay

Drive

Mesa Lane

Escalona Dr.

King Street

Mission Street

King St.

1

Mission

St.

Swift Street

Natural Bridges Dr.

Start
Here

NATURAL BRIDGES
STATE BEACH

# 32 APTOS SEA-TREE TOUR

**General location: Santa Cruz - Aptos**
**Distance: 29 miles**
**Riding time: 2 - 4 hours**
**Road/Traffic conditions: Very good/Moderate**
**Facilities: Aptos, Watsonville, Freedom, Cor-**
**ralitos**
**Ride rating: ***

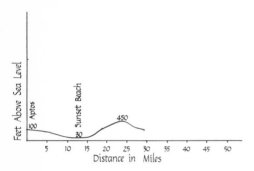

The small beach town of Aptos is only about 7 miles south of Santa Cruz on State Highway 1. To reach the starting point of this trip, take the Seacliff Beach - Aptos exit from State Highway 1 and then go left across the overpass toward the town of Aptos. After turning right on Soquel Drive you will see a large shopping center on your right hand side. This is a good place to begin cycling. This circle ride is quite long and you will find a number of hills along the route. The hills are quite gradual for the most part, since the ride route stays near sea level most of the way. It would be wise to carry a warm sweater or jacket on this trip, regardless of the time of year, since temperatures along the coast can sometimes be quite cool. Only a few miles inland, however, near Watsonville and Corralitos, it can become very warm.

Aptos, an Indian word meaning "meeting of the streams", is a quiet little town which was once a fashionable resort. In the 1800's Claus Spreckels, founder of California's first sugar dynasty, located his impressive estate here, complete with a race track and a large mansion containing an elevator. Spreckels managed his sugar beet refinery in nearby Watsonville from his home in Aptos where he entertained important visitors such as the king of the Hawaiian Islands.

After you glide down San Andreas Road past the community of La Selva Beach and Manresa Beach State Park you will pass by fields of fragrant flowers and acres of brussel sprouts and squash. Soon you will approach Sunset Beach State Park, a 7 mile long sandy beach with hundreds of rolling sand dunes and high bluffs. Bicyclists are permitted here and swimming is excellent during the summer months. You may find more fog here in the summer than you would a few miles north at Seacliff or Natural Bridges, but the weather is usually mild. Sunset Beach stretches to the Pajaro River on the south, which was named Rio del Pajaro (river of the bird) by the Portola expedition in the late 1700's because they found on its banks a great eagle stuffed with straw which had been put there by the local Indians. The road at the southern end of Sunset Beach State Park is blocked to automobile traffic, but the wily cyclist will have no problem scooting past the gates on Shell Drive to Beach Road which goes northeast or left toward Watsonville. On Beach Road about two miles from Watsonville you will pass an old white mansion with some rather bizarre, intricately sculptured bushes in front of the house. The mansion is over 100 years old, and the bush with "U.S.A." was clipped and shaped in 1927 commemorating Lindbergh's first trans-Atlantic airplane flight. Other bushes show the names of some of the past residents of the house.

You will cycle through Watsonville before beginning your return trip to Aptos via Freedom and Corralitos. Watsonville has been called the strawberry capital of the world, although it is also a growing and canning center for many fruits and vegetables, including apples, apricots, lettuce, artichokes, cider and vinegar. Watsonville's plaza was once the scene of bull and bear fights, and horse racing was common on the main street in the days when townsmen spent their Sundays, after dutifully attending church, gambling, dancing and carousing. Beyond Watsonville and nearby Freedom the countryside is covered with thousands of apple trees. The orchards are snowy with blossoms in the springtime and luxuriantly green in the summer.

The trees, drooping under the burden of their fruit, are propped up to keep their branches from breaking in late summer. Along the way you will probably pass little roadside stands selling cold cider and in the fall when the apples are picked, fresh apples and apple juice are sold along the route. The smell of this fresh-picked fruit from the orchards and the juicing houses permeates the fall air.

From Corralitos on Hames Road and Freedom Boulevard, the ride becomes a bit more hilly as you move through more of the orchard covered slopes, until you reach Soquel Drive and the short return to your starting point.

*Sculptured Bushes*

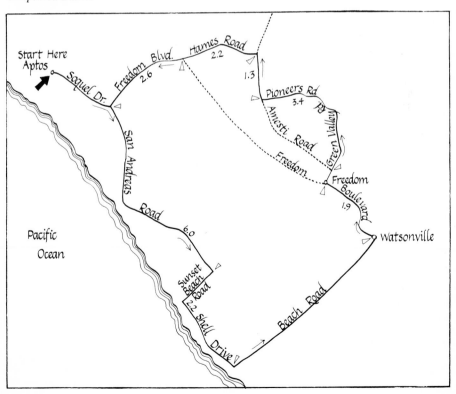

# 33 PAJARO PUSSYFOOT

**General location: Watsonville - Pajaro**
**Distance: 21 miles round trip**
**Riding time: 2 - 3 hours**
**Road/Traffic conditions: Very good/Light moderate**
**Facilities: Small store on Elkhorn Road; picnicking — Kirby Park, Elkhorn Slough**
**Ride rating: * ***

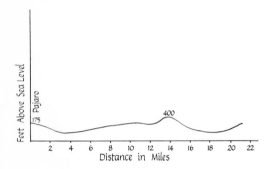

This ride, south of Watsonville and Pajaro, winds through the heart of some relatively flat ranch land only a few miles from the Pacific. The actual starting point is at the Pajaro Valley Golf Club on Salinas Road east of State Highway 1.

You'll ride east only one-half mile or so before turning right or south on G12, a county road. Stay on this road for only a brief time before Hall Road (G12) goes left and Elkhorn Road, your route, branches to the right. You'll go down Elkhorn Road for about 7 miles through the marshy lands bordering expansive Elkhorn Slough. To the west, on the ocean, you will undoubtedly see the industrial complex at Moss Landing. Since California's early days, this has been a busy fishing and industrial center. The little village was established in 1865 by Captain Charles Moss and up until 1920 as many as five whales a week were

processed here, despite complaints of inhabitants for miles around as the odors drifted inland. The Elkhorn Slough running to the Pacific at Moss Landing is a refuge for many varieties of ocean birds which you may see at Kirby Park, a fishing and recreational area on the Elkhorn Road. A peculiar type of marine algae in the slough makes the water reddish.

The terrain becomes more rolling and more heavily wooded near the end of the Elkhorn Road and for most of the remainder of the trip. However, these hills are not long and are not particularly steep. The roads you will follow back toward Pajaro proceed past small farms and ranches, old ramshackle frame buildings and a few small residential communities. The route is a very enjoyable one, usually warm and clear, which helps make cycling conditions ideal.

*Old O.K. Hatchery near Pajaro*

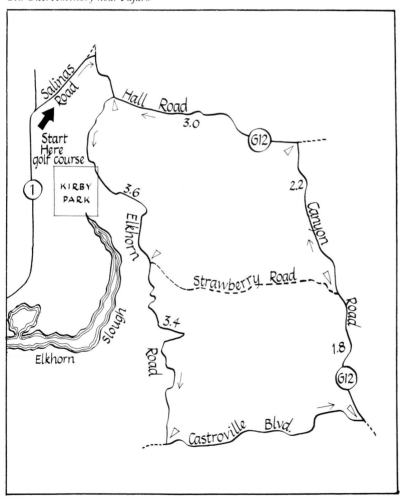

# 34 SAN JUAN BAUTISTA

General location: Between Gilroy and Salinas
   off of U.S. 101
Distance: 9 miles round trip
Riding time: 45 minutes
Road/Traffic conditions: Very good/Moderate
Facilities: San Juan Bautista
Ride rating: *

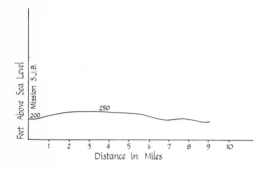

San Juan Bautista is located south of
Gilroy just off U.S. 101. To reach the
town, take State Highway 156 2.5 miles
east from U.S. 101 toward Hollister.

This short, flat ride around San Juan
will give the cyclist a great view of this
agricultural area and the mountains surrounding this peaceful little mission
town. For the most part, except for a
short section on State Highway 156,
traffic is light. Highway 156, even though
more heavily traveled, has a wide, paved
shoulder and offers no real safety hazard.
San Juan Bautista has several points of
historical interest, most of which are included in the superb State Historical
Park located here. San Juan is the site
of one of California's 21 Franciscan missions. It was the rallying point of two
revolutions and was the setting for
Alfred Hitchcock's movie "Vertigo."

The mission, founded in 1797, is the
oldest historic building facing the central
plaza. It was started by Padre Fermin
Francisco de Lasuen because of its stra-
tegic location relative to other missions,
the many Indians in the area and the
excellent soil, good water supply and
plentiful building materials. At one
time over 1200 Indians lived and worked
at the mission and more than 4300 Indians are buried in the old cemetery
beside the northeast wall of the mission

church. Despite damage from numerous
earthquakes throughout the years, the
church has been used since 1812.

A small portion of El Camino Real can
be seen from the Indian cemetery at the
northeast end of the mission. This is the
"King's Highway" that connected all of
the California missions and later served
as one of California's major stage and
wagon roads. Today, many of our modern
highways follow the El Camino in northern and southern California.

On Second Street facing the plaza are
two interesting buildings which have been
renovated and preserved as part of the
California State Historic Park (the mission still belongs to the Catholic Church
and is not a part of the state park). The
Castro House once belonged to Jose
Maria Castro, the most prominent Castro
in California history. He was twice
acting governor of the northern half of
Alta California and was prominent in
the Spanish military during the early
1800's. The Castro House today has
been furnished in the style of the 1870's
when it was owned by the Breen family,
survivors of the ill-fated Donner Party.
The Plaza Hotel, next to the Castro
Adobe, has been restored to its 1870's
appearance when it was owned by Angelo
Zanetta. Zanetta, an Italian, was a pro-
fessional restauranteur and hotel man
and established the Plaza Hotel as an
excellent eating and stopping-off point
for travelers. Zanetta added the second
story to the Hotel in 1858, shortly after
he purchased the original building and
site.

The Plaza Stables, Zanetta House and
Zanetta cottage are located on the eastern
side of the Plaza. The stables, as can be
imagined by its great size and beautifully
restored contents, did a large business
in the 1860's and 1870's. As many as
11 stages arrived and departed daily
when seven stage lines operated in San
Juan. The town was an important stopping place for freight and travelers from
San Francisco to Los Angeles and between the San Benito Mountain quick-
silver mines and Hollister, Watsonville,
Monterey and Santa Cruz. When, in
1876, the railroad bypassed San Juan,
the little town's boom years were over.

The Zanetta House, acquired by Zanetta in 1868, was laid out as a private residence on the bottom floor, now beautifully preserved with priceless furniture and personal items of clothing. The top floor was a public meeting hall for celebrations, political rallies and shows.

Just off the plaza near the Zanetta House is a delightful wine tasting room operated by the Almaden Vineyards. Picnic tables, some picnic supplies and, of course, the wine of your choice are available here should you care to have a leisurely lunch and a relaxing siesta on the beautiful green plaza lawn. In the main part of town on Third Street are many very interesting antique, art, and novelty shops and several restaurants.

*Plaza Hotel at San Juan Bautista*

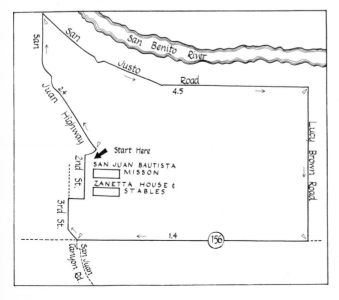

**General location:** Monterey Peninsula - Carmel
**Distance:** 18 miles full circle from Pacific Grove Gate (remember to stay on orange and yellow lined road). Flat alternate route for those wishing to avoid climbing Huckleberry Hill: Pacific Grove to Carmel City Gate, or vice versa, down and back, 18 miles.
**Riding time:** 2 - 3 hours
**Road/Traffic conditions:** Good; rough in places/Moderate; since the traffic at all of the gates is routed right, less traffic will be encountered by going left.
**Facilities:** Restrooms — Bird Rock, Del Monte Lodge; refreshments, soda fountain, grocery store at Del Monte Lodge.
**Ride rating:** ✱✱

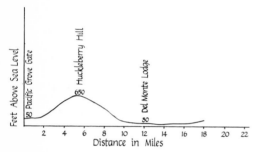

*NOTE:* Recent restrictions in bicycling on the 17 Mile Drive by the Del Monte Properties Company may limit your weekend bicycling plans for this ride. Briefly, the restrictions include the following:

1. Restriction of bicycle traffic on weekends and holidays to responsible cyclists in recognized organizations and clubs. Group permission to ride on weekends and holidays must be obtained in advance by writing:

> Security Office
> Del Monte Properties Company
> P.O. Box 567
> Pebble Beach, Calif. 93953

2. The restriction is in effect on weekends, holidays and for special events (like the Crosby Golf Classic), but is not in effect at other times. The restriction is based on the company's ". . . moral obligation to reduce the possibility of accidents and injuries within the Forest."

The Del Monte Properties Company claims that their restrictions are a result of some recent bicycle accidents in heavy weekend traffic. They have mentioned a number of alternatives which have been considered, such as the building of bicycle paths, restriction of automobile traffic and/or a charge for visiting cyclists. None of the alternatives have been deemed acceptable by the company to date while the "experimental" restrictions, as described above, continue to be in effect.

For convenient parking, the Pacific Grove Gate or the Carmel City Gate are the most ideal places to start this ride. The Carmel Hill gate, the only other entrance to 17 Mile Drive, does not have parking. Bicycling through the gates, as opposed to driving through, will save you the $3 auto entry fee.

The Pacific Grove Gate is most easily reached by taking Coast Highway 1 to State Highway 68 toward Monterey and Pacific Grove. The other recommended entry to this ride is the Carmel City Gate which can be reached by turning west off Highway 1 on Ocean Avenue just south of the Carmel Hill Gate - Highway 68 turnoff. By turning right on North San Antonio Avenue at the foot of Ocean Avenue (a block from Carmel Beach) you can easily reach the City Gate entry to the 17 Mile Drive.

The Del Monte Forest, which is circled by the 17 Mile Drive, is a private park with a magnificent panorama of incomparable beauty. From crashing surf on the craggy shores of Cypress Point and Bird Rock to the lofty wooded knolls overlooking Pacific Grove and Monterey Bay, this carefully protected area provides a fascinating spectrum of wildlife and natural beauty.

*Regular Route:* If you begin cycling at the Pacific Grove Gate and decide to go to the left on the 17 Mile Drive, you will climb Huckleberry Hill, one of the highest points in Del Monte Forest. This hill is 4 miles long and is quite steep in places. A 10-speed bicycle with low or alpine gearing would be helpful. Once atop Huckleberry Hill, however, you'll experience not only a superb view of the ocean and surrounding area but also an exhilarating ride down toward Carmel and the Del Monte Lodge. Del Monte Forest picnic grounds on Huckleberry Hill is a good place for a lunch break.

*Alternate Route:* Some of the most breath-taking points of interest on this route are located along the coast between the Pacific Grove Gate and the Carmel City Gate. This is a rather flat portion of the 17 Mile Drive, running along the ocean most of the way, and may be a more desirable alternative to many cyclists who don't want to face the hilly challenge of the complete 17 Mile Drive loop. This route, from the Pacific Grove to Carmel City Gate (or vice versa) is about an 18 mile round trip.

Just inside the Pacific Grove Gate on this route you'll see a beach sand production plant owned by the Del Monte Properties Co., and on the coast, Point Joe, named after a Japanese squatter who lived there many years. Point Joe has been the scene of several disastrous shipwrecks in California history, partly due to the fact that it has been mistaken as the entrance to Monterey Bay. Shortly after passing Point Joe, moving south along the ocean, you'll cycle through Monterey Peninsula Golf Course before reaching Seal and Bird Rocks, home of seals, sea lions, cormorants and sea gulls.

A vista point and circular tourist information building is located here.

Immediately south of the Bird Rock observation area you'll pass by Spyglass Hill and Cypress Point Golf courses and then past the turnoff to Point Cypress vista point, which is only 0.1 mile off the 17 Mile Drive. Pressing on toward the Del Monte Lodge and the Pebble Beach Golf Course you'll come upon some of the area's famous twisted, wind-tortured cypress trees. The Lone Cypress Tree near Midway Point is perhaps the most painted and photographed in the forest. The Ghost Tree and Witch Tree at Pescadero Point are bleached almost white and are strangely contorted from years of wear by ocean winds and spray. In this area you will also ride by some of the area's magnificent private residences.

Two other noteworthy points of interest along the coast before reaching the City Gate are the Del Monte Lodge and the famous Pebble Beach Golf Course.

The Carmel and Monterey coastline area is often cool, breezy and/or foggy. It is advisable to always carry warm clothing when cycling in this area.

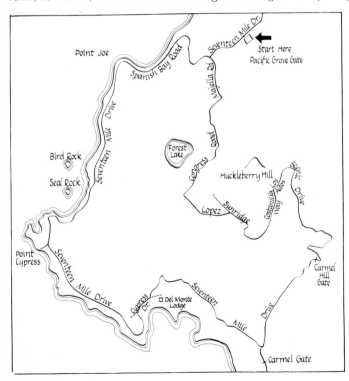

# 36 CARMEL VALLEY

General location: Carmel - Monterey
Distance: 23.6 miles to Carmel Valley and back
Riding time: 2 - 3 hours
Road/Traffic conditions: Very good/Moderate -
  heavy
Facilities: shopping center at trip start; Carmel
  Valley
Ride rating: * *

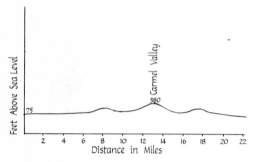

The relatively flat, scenic trip from Carmel to the little village of Carmel Valley is most conveniently begun at the large shopping center about 0.5 mile east of State Highway 1 on Carmel Valley Road (G16). From this shopping center Carmel Valley Road climbs very gradually to Carmel Valley, about 12 miles away. The beginning elevation at the shopping center is only 100' and Carmel Valley is 383' so the up and back trip can generally be described as gradual up, gradual down, with very few intervening hills of any consequence.

Carmel Valley Road follows the Carmel River as it wanders through the farms, orchards and pastures of the valley. This popular inland area, which has more sunshine, warmer temperatures and less fog than the area immediately surrounding Carmel, is rapidly becoming more populated. The building of golf courses, shopping areas, retirement centers and ranch homes highlight the dynamic growth of this area.

This ride along the peaceful Carmel River between the chaparral of the Santa Lucia Mountains is very pleasant. You will pass Pinyon Peak (2237') on your right as you approach Carmel Valley. To the south of Carmel Valley lies San Clemente Reservoir on the Carmel River. The river flows from the expansive Los Padres National Forest and Ventana Wilderness Area only 10 miles to the south. The Carmel River holds trout and steelhead, and during the spawning season steelhead are plentiful in the river. The Santa Lucia mountains are known for their wild boar and deer hunting.

There are many good picnic sites along the Carmel River should you care to stop, relax and eat lunch. All in all, the up and back jaunt to Carmel Valley offers a bit warmer, drier, less blustery alternative to riding on or near the coast on the Monterey Peninsula. Whether or not the weather there is cold or foggy, riding to Carmel Valley can be an invigorating, beautiful trip.

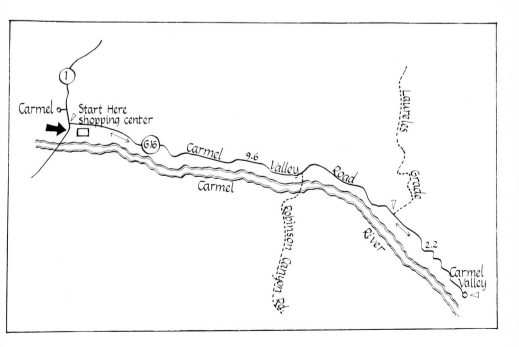

# 37 CARMEL BEACH AND MISSION RIDE

**General location: Monterey - Carmel**
**Distance: 4 miles round trip**
**Riding time: ½ - 1 hour**
**Road/Traffic conditions: Narrow in places on Scenic Road/Moderate-heavy traffic on weekends**
**Facilities: Town of Carmel**
**Ride rating: ***

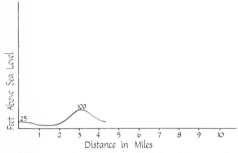

The starting point of this ride can be reached by turning west on Ocean Avenue from Coast Highway 1 toward the town of Carmel. Go to the foot of Ocean Avenue (on Carmel Bay), where parking is usually adequate, and begin the ride here by going south on Scenic Road.

This ride is a short and exhilarating loop on the western and southern borders of Carmel. This brief circle tour is an ideal way to start the day — a relaxing, picturesque and appetite-building prelude to a hearty breakfast. The route first takes you along Carmel's dazzling white beach, then along the northern edge of the Carmel River State Beach, and finally, by the famous Carmel Mission, before returning through a pleasant residential area to Ocean Avenue, the main street of Carmel.

Although the water of Carmel Bay is unsafe for swimming and is also very cold, a few brave surfers can usually be seen off shore wearing their wetsuits and waiting for the perfect wave. The beach is more of a place for sunbathing, congregating with friends, or just walking and enjoying the sunshine and fresh sea breeze. You'll enjoy the view of the beach from the Scenic Road which is amply lined with dark gnarled cypress trees. At the southern end of Carmel Beach in Carmel River State Park the shoreline becomes craggy and rough and the waves

pound the shore in white, foamy fury.

In the state park, as Scenic Road turns eastward, you can, if you wish, picnic around a beach fire, investigate nearby tide pools, or splash in the Carmel River as it enters the bay.

Further on, near Junipero Avenue, is Mission San Carlos Borromeo del Rio Carmelo, founded in 1770, and from which the town was named. This mission is the final resting place and was the home of Father Junipero Serra who was an explorer, traveler and founder of nine early California missions. He was instrumental in moving the mission from its original site in Monterey to its present location on the Carmel River in 1770-71. The mission grounds, museums, memorial and church are open to the public and offer a glimpse into an interesting part of early California history.

From the mission, ride north on Junipero Avenue through a beautifully green, heavily-wooded portion of residential Carmel to Ocean Avenue. It's an extremely pleasant experience to coast down Ocean Avenue through quaint Carmel-by-the-Sea, especially when you can escape from being trapped in the oftentimes heavy village traffic.

The Carmel-Monterey area is often cool, breezy and/or foggy. It's advisable to carry warm clothing when cycling in this area.

*Carmel Mission*

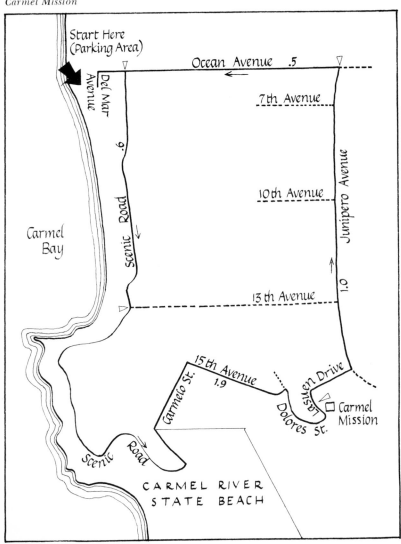

Start Here
(Parking Area)

Del Mar Avenue

Ocean Avenue   .5

7th Avenue

Junipero Avenue

10th Avenue

.9

Scenic Road

Carmel
Bay

1.0

13th Avenue

15th Avenue
1.9

Carmelo St.

Lasuen Drive

Dolores St.

Carmel
Mission

Scenic Road

CARMEL RIVER
STATE BEACH

# 38 TYLER ISLAND TULE

**General location:** Sacramento River Delta - Rio Vista
**Distance:** 16.7 miles round trip
**Riding time:** 1 - 2 hours
**Road/Traffic conditions:** Excellent but narrow on levees/Light
**Facilities:** Isleton
**Ride rating:** **

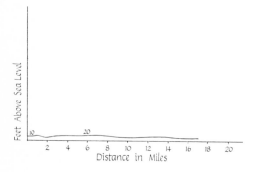

The Tyler Island Bridge Road near the town of Isleton is the pushing off point for this trip. Isleton is just north of Rio Vista and can be reached by going north on State Highway 160 at Rio Vista. Isleton is located between the major cities of Antioch and Pittsburgh to the south and Sacramento to the north. Highway 160 (Isleton Road) junctions with Tyler Island Bridge Road 1.5 miles north of Isleton. A large area on the west side of Isleton Road provides ample parking for riders driving to this starting point.

Tyler Island Road is built on a levee. Most levees exist for the purpose of keeping the river within its banks and many of the levees along the Sacramento River were projects of the U.S. Army Corps of Engineers. Levee roads, as a rule, are narrow with steep embankments on either side. Cyclists should avoid riding too close to the edge of the levee roads since the shoulders are either very narrow or nonexistent. Traffic on Tyler

Island is very light and cycling is quite safe. In addition, traffic moves slowly on this road and cyclists are clearly visible.

In the waterways around the island you will see a myriad of house boats, speed boats and sailboats. Fishermen, lounging lazily beside the slough or river, may remind you of the scenes described by Mark Twain in his adventures of Tom Sawyer and Huck Finn. The pace of life on the sloughs (pronounced sloo), rivers and levee roads changes from the frenzied urban rat race which you may be used to to a noiseless, slow-moving and thoroughly relaxing life-tempo. There is absolutely no threat of heavy crossroad or major thoroughfare traffic on this trip. The land is very flat which, of course, means that you can ride more steadily and tirelessly but still be able to set a pace which will give you the right amount of exercise. The nature of this ride makes it very suitable for a family outing.

Isleton is a farming, trading, and canning center which is especially known for its production of canned asparagus, which has been estimated at about 90 percent of the world's supply.

The tule-fringed Georgiana Slough and Mokelumne River bordering Tyler Island are the marshy homes of ducks during the migration season — chiefly mallard, green winged teal and sprig. Other birds are also found here — the Wilson snipe, spoonbill, red-head wigeon and canvas back duck.

The weather in the delta is usually quite warm and muggy in summer months. Fall and spring months bring more moderate temperatures, but it is possible to enjoy year round cycling here.

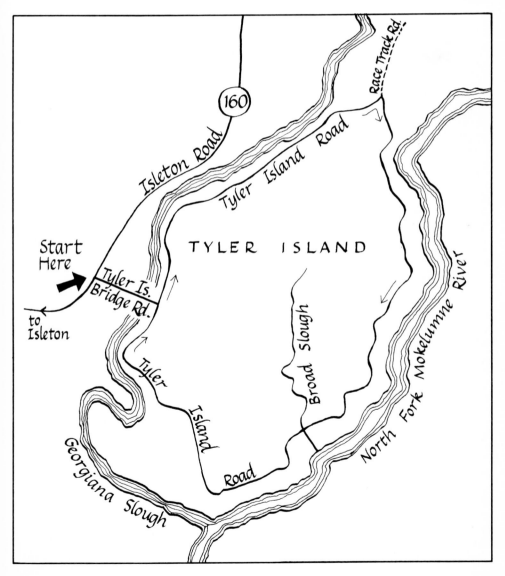

# 39 RYER ISLAND — RYDE RIDE

**General location:** Sacramento River Delta - Rio Vista
**Distance:** 23.8 miles round trip
**Riding time:** 1½ - 3 hours
**Road/Traffic conditions:** Excellent but narrow on levees/very little traffic
**Facilities:** Food, drink at Howard Landing, Walker Landing, Ryde; picnicking at Hogback Island Recreation Area
**Ride rating:** **

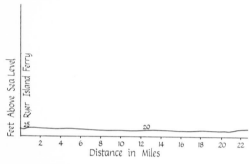

The town of Rio Vista, near the starting point of this very flat, very enjoyable ride, can be reached by taking State Highway 12 or State Highways 160 and 12. Rio Vista, called the Beverly Hills of Northern California by Erle Stanley Gardner, is located between the major cities of Antioch and Pittsburgh to the south and Sacramento to the north. Take the road to Ryer Island on the west end of the Rio Vista bridge crossing the Sacramento River. This road goes north 2.5 miles to the Ryer Island Ferry crossing over Cache Slough. The designated start of this ride is immediately before the Ryer Island Ferry crossing.

After you cross the Ryer Island Ferry you may have your first experience in riding on a levee road. (The ferries in the Delta area are state operated and there is no charge for crossing.) The roads on the levees (embankments on the shores of rivers to protect against flood) are quite narrow with a steep embankment on either side. Care should be exercised in not wandering too close to the edge of the road since there are no shoulders. But since traffic on these delta "islands" is so light, there is little danger of being forced off the road by motorized vehicles. In addition, the speed of the traffic on the levee roads is quite leisurely and cyclists are clearly visible.

The road on Ryer Island is very flat. On the shores of Cache Slough, as you proceed north on Ryer Island, you will undoubtedly see many people lazily fishing, a la Mark Twain or Dutch canal style, and relaxing in deck chairs or having a picnic lunch. There's a Huck Finnish sort of feeling that pervades your soul in the delta area. Life seems to move more slowly and people take the time to call out a cheerful greeting. It's almost like you're in another part of the country. The delta country definitely has an atmosphere all its own.

Imagine this trip as a figure eight laying on its side. The midpoint or crisscross portion of the figure eight is at the Howard Landing Ferry where, on your eastward journey you will cross the Steamboat Slough and ride toward Walker Landing and then on toward Ryde. On the return, westward trip, the crossing of Steamboat Slough will again be made at Howard Landing Ferry but you should turn left immediately on Ryer Road East and ride along the eastern side of Ryer Island on Steamboat Slough. Ryer Road East will take you back to the Ryer Island Ferry and your starting point.

The prize most fishermen hope to take from the brackish waters of the sloughs and rivers in the delta are striped bass. The waterways in the delta region are influenced by the tides of San Francisco Bay and actually change level corresponding to ocean tidal fluctuations. The land on Ryer Island is primarily used for agricultural purposes and a variety of crops can usually be seen alongside the road. The flat farmland also make this area an ideal habitat for pheasants, quail and other bird life which can usually be seen from the levee roads.

After crossing Steamboat Slough and proceeding toward Walker Landing you will have an opportunity to picnic in a very pretty, grassy, well-cared-for park just south of Walker Landing Road. The park is called the Hogback Island Recreational Facility and is also used for boat launching. In case you didn't bring a lunch along there is a little grocery store on the road from Ryde just after disembarking from the Howard Landing Ferry.

*Ryer Island*

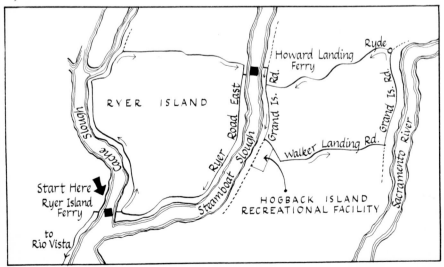

# 40 ANDRUS ISLAND

**General location:** Sacramento River Delta - Isleton
**Distance:** 14.4 miles round trip
**Riding time:** 1 - 2 hours
**Road/Traffic conditions:** Excellent/Light - moderate
**Facilities:** Isleton
**Ride rating:** *

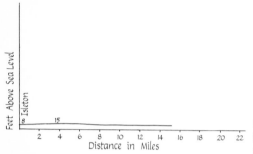

The town of Isleton can be reached by taking State Highway 160 north from Pittsburgh and Antioch or south from Sacramento. Isleton is about 4 miles north of Rio Vista on the Sacramento River.

Like the other island rides in the Sacramento River delta region, this ride is very flat. It is also like the other recommended delta rides in that the route laid out follows the levee roads for most of the way. All of these levees exist for the purpose of keeping the rivers or sloughs within their banks. The roads on top of the levees are usually narrow with steep embankments on both sides, so care should be taken in not riding too close to the edge. These roads are usually lightly traveled by automobiles, traffic is slow, and cyclists are clearly visible.

The roads around Andrus Island follow two small sloughs, the Jackson and Georgiana Sloughs and two good sized rivers, the San Joaquin and Mokelumne. This ride will take you through the center of some of the typical river delta resort areas including extensive boat docking and storage facilities, boat launching and rental areas and restaurants. This does not mean that this ride is characterized by a conglomeration of commercialism. There is much quiet country especially on Jackson Sough Road, but the San Joaquin and Mokelumne Rivers bring more boats, more people and more of a hustle-bustle to the normally slow-moving delta lowlands. In the waterways around the island you will see a wide variety of boats, both the simple and the elegant, from 30-foot sailboats and large power boats to small outboards and rowboats. Watching the marine traffic as you ride along the levees is always fascinating. This area also draws fishermen in great numbers.

Isleton, the starting point of this ride is a farming, trading and canning center and is especially known for its asparagus production, which has been estimated at about 90 percent of the world's supply. Old frame and brick storefronts, weathered and in disrepair, face the street. Many of the buildings have oriental writing on their fronts. Old men clustered in small groups chat and gesture unhurriedly or simply watch traffic and pedestrians pass by on the street. Isleton has many of the characteristics of other quaint oriental delta towns on the Sacramento River like the very old Chinese town of Locke with its narrow main street and weathered two-story frame buildings, which is only about 10 miles further north on State Highway 160.

The tule-fringed Jackson Slough and Mokelumne River bordering Andrus Island are the marshy homes of many types of ducks during the migration season — chiefly mallard, green winged teal and sprig.

The weather in the delta region is usually quite warm in summer months. Fall and spring are more moderate in temperature, but regardless of season, it is possible to enjoy good cycling here year round.

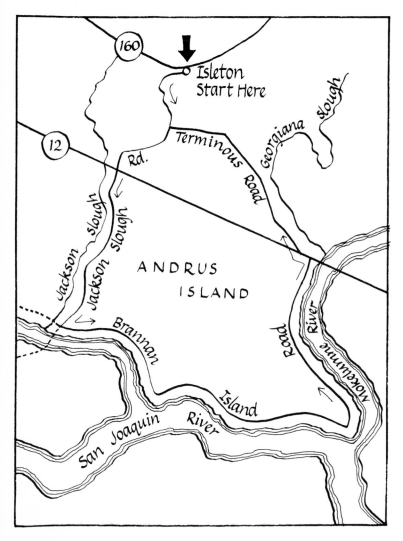

# 41 SACRAMENTO — AMERICAN RIVER BIKE WAY

**General location: Sacramento**
**Distance: 12 miles round trip**
**Riding time: 1 - 2 hours**
**Road/Traffic conditions: Excellent/Light**
**Facilities: Picnicking, vendors in Discovery Park**
**Ride rating: ***

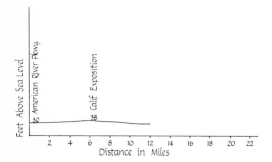

Discovery Park in the American River Parkway is the starting point for this bikeway ride up the American River toward the California Exposition, which is also part of the American River Parkway. Discovery Park is located just off Interstate Highway 5 between Interstate 80 to the south and Interstate 880 to the north. Take the Garden Highway exit east off Interstate 5 to Discovery Park Road and the entrance to the park.

This is a very flat ride along the Natomas East Main Drainage Canal and then along the American River toward the California Exposition. Since there is no automobile traffic and the bikeway is located along a very scenic portion of the river, this short ride is most enjoyable. It is very safe and is recommended for all members of the family.

Discovery Park is located at the confluence of the Sacramento and American Rivers in West Sacramento. In the park, at the beginning of the bikeway, stands a sign describing the American River Bikeway and a small wooden sign signaling "Mile 0". Mileage markers have been placed along the full length of the bikeway. The American River Bikeway is completely paved and is in excellent condition. It begins by wiggling under an Interstate 5 overpass and skirting the southern side of the Natomas East Drainage Canal. The area surrounding the bikeway is heavily wooded and has retained a natural river country appearance in spite of its nearness to the heart of Sacramento. The only words of caution, as you follow the American River Bikeway, is to take care in avoiding collisions with other cyclists, who are especially numerous on weekends. The bikeway is wide enough to allow plenty of room for passing other bikes or pedestrians. Along the route you will see some very nice areas for picnics as well as river beaches for relaxing or sunning.

The Sacramento area is becoming well known for its pioneering efforts in the development of safe, well-conceived and well-constructed bikeways. The town of Davis is probably the best known in the area for its bike path engineering.

*American River Bike Way*

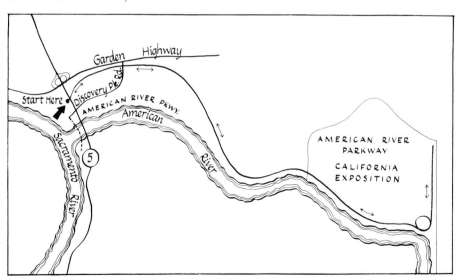

## FOLSOM — "WHERE THE WEST CAME AND STAYED"

General location: Sacramento
Distance: 11.5 miles round trip
Riding time: 1 - 2 hours
Road/Traffic conditions: Very good/Moderate
Facilities: Folsom
Ride rating: *

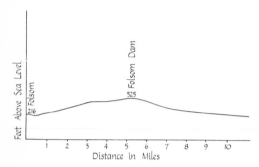

Historic Folsom, located about 20 miles northeast of Sacramento, is the starting point of this short circle tour. Folsom can be reached by taking Folsom Boulevard north from U.S. 50.

This trip, beginning in the frontier-like settlement of Folsom, has one rather gradual, but quite long hill going from the village to Folsom Lake and Dam. The outskirts of Folsom are quickly reached at the junction of Placerville and Blue Ravine Roads. The countryside after this point is very quiet and idyllic. After crossing the dam, the road then goes downward toward Negro Bar on the American River.

The little town of Folsom is characterized as a real western town. Rows of brick and frame buildings face each other on the mall on historic Sutter Street. Nearby is the old Southern Pacific Depot and the old powerhouse, located near Negro Bar. This town had its beginnings in the 1850's and 1860's when the state experienced a hugh flow of gold and fortune seekers. Negro Bar, which you will pass by just before you cross the American River on Rainbow Bridge on the return trip, is now part of Folsom State Park. Here, in 1849, Negro miners dug for gold and established a camp.

The land around and including the town of Folsom was first granted to William Leidesdorff, a U.S. vice-consul in 1844. In 1848, Captain Joseph L. Folsom bought the 35,000 acres from Leidesdorff. This land and other property acquired in San Francisco soon made Folsom one of California's richest men.

The town of Folsom also became known early in California history as an important railroad supply depot for the mining country and as an important stopping off point for the Pony Express. Folsom prides itself today on its historical tradition as well as its "Biggest Little Zoo" and "Scenic Railroad" located in a small well-kept city park on northern Natoma Street. Folsom is also known for the Folsom State Penitentiary which is not visible on the ride. The penitentiary is on the south bank of the American River (see map) and was built in 1880. The structure is a fortress-like building surrounded by the fertile land near the river.

The Folsom Lake State Recreation Area includes Folsom Lake, Negro Bar west of Folsom and Lake Natoma to the south. It is reputed to be the most popular multi-use and year-round park in the state. The park is the scene of a great variety of recreational activities among which include fishing, boating, hiking, camping, picnicking, horseback riding, swimming and water skiing. Folsom Lake, beyond the dam you will cycle across, has 120 miles of shoreline. The dams at Folsom and Natoma Lakes control the waters of the American River to protect downstream communities from flood. The stored water is a source of power and is also used for irrigation.

Fishermen in the park attempt to catch the wily trout, catfish, large and small mouth bass, perch and sturgeon. There are good camping facilities in many areas of the park — at Negro Bar, Beals Point, and Peninsula Campground.

*Main Street in Old Folsom*

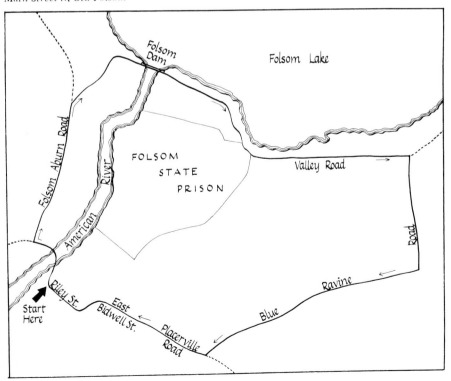

# 43 UNIVERSITY OF THE PACIFIC — EIGHT MILE ROAD RIDE

**General location: Stockton, University of the Pacific**
**Distance: 33.5 miles to the end and back**
**Riding time: 2½ - 4 hours**
**Road/Traffic conditions: Very good/Moderate**
**Facilities: Stockton; Helen & Herman's at turnaround point**
**Ride rating: * * ***

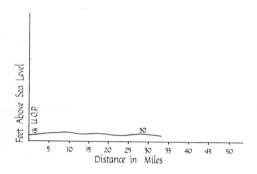

Although the distance of this ride makes it a more difficult one, it is *very* flat, and given enough time, most cyclists could complete this trip.

The starting point for the ride is on the University of the Pacific campus between the major arterial streets of Pershing Avenue to the west and Pacific Avenue to the east. A good place to begin is at the end of Baxter Way on the campus, just before a little bridge that crosses the Calaveras River. A very nice Stockton (paved) bikeway follows along the west side of Pershing Avenue for a short distance before reaching Hammer Lane. The ride from Davis Road to the turnaround point on Eight Mile Road is a pleasant farmland ride crossing some of the islands in the river delta area.

The city of Stockton in the heart of San Joaquin Valley's agricultural region is California's major inland seaport shipping about 85 percent of the grain exported by California and is the principal shipping port for such major crops as asparagus, tomatoes, Tokay grapes, potatoes, celery, and cherries. The San Joaquin and Calaveras Rivers border the city and

the Stockton Deep Water Channel cuts through the city, stopping at its center.

Historically, Stockton was a major gold rush town in the mid-1800's. Bayard Taylor, noted author and traveler, found Stockton in 1849 ". . . a canvas town of a thousand inhabitants and a port with 25 vessels at anchor! . . . — the click of hammers and the grating of saws — the shouts of mule drivers — the jingling of spurs — the jar and jostle of wares in the tents — almost cheated me into the belief that it was some old commercial mart. . . Four months had sufficed to make the place what it was." By 1853 Stockton's population had grown from a few hundred to 5000 inhabitants. As the gold rush boom diminished, irrigation of the fertile farmlands was introduced and Stockton began to firmly establish itself as the Valley's major agricultural center.

University of the Pacific was established by the Methodist Church in San Jose in 1851 and was California's first chartered institution of higher learning. The college was moved to Stockton in 1924. The chapel tower on the campus is one of the area's principal landmarks.

*Foot Bridge at U.O.P.*

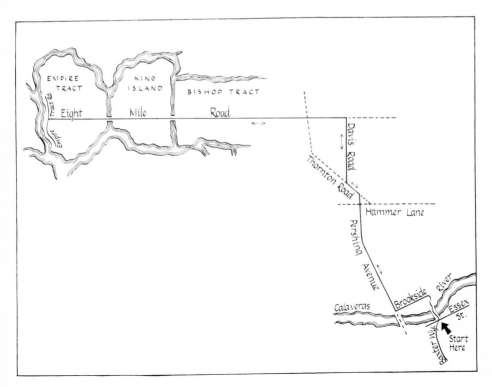

# 44 STOCKTON TO MICKE GROVE

**General location:** Stockton, University of the Pacific
**Distance:** 21 miles round trip
**Riding time:** 1½ - 3 hours
**Road/Traffic conditions:** Very good/Moderate
**Facilities:** Stockton, Micke Grove
**Ride rating:** ★★

*Micke's Grove*

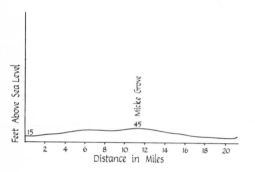

The goal of this trip is to reach Micke Grove Park which is north of Stockton and only about 5 miles south of Lodi. This figure eight loop is a little more than 10 flat miles each way from the starting point at University of the Pacific in Stockton. The starting point for the ride is at the end of Baxter Way between Pershing and Pacific Avenues on the U.O.P. campus. Here, where Baxter Way ends, a pleasant foot and bicycle bridge crosses the Calaveras River. A very enjoyable paved bikeway exists, on the west side of the street, on Pershing Avenue between Brookside Road and Hammer Lane. Although the bikeway is quite short, it does exist solely for pedestrians and cyclists and provides a safer alternative than riding in the Stockton traffic.

The city of Stockton is in the middle of some very fertile, prosperous farmland in the San Joaquin Valley. Stockton is California's major inland seaport and ships about 85 percent of the grain exported by California each year. Other agricultural products like asparagus, tomatoes, Tokay grapes, potatoes, celery and cherries are shipped from the port.

In early California history, Stockton was near the Mother Lode area and experienced much of the same growing pains as many of the gold rush towns. Stockton grew from a tent village with a few hundred people to a thriving city of over 5000 in only a matter of months. But Stockton didn't suffer the same fate as many of the mining towns which became ghost towns after depleting their supply of precious metal. The fertile farming land, irrigation and river access to markets helped Stockton grow into the agricultural center it is today.

The University of the Pacific, at the starting point of the ride, was first started in San Jose in 1851 by the Methodist Church. This makes it California's first chartered institution of higher education. Since 1924 the school has been in Stockton and is the city's major college.

Popular Micke Grove is the turnaround and resting point of this trip. This 59 acre grove was the gift of the late William C. Micke, Lodi vineyardist, to the San Joaquin County Park system. It contains one of the few remaining natural stands of native valley oak. Here you will find a neat, well-maintained zoo, beautiful camelia and Japanese gardens, a small amusement park, picnic tables, grassy recreation areas and a snack bar. It's a busy place on weekends when Lodi and Stockton residents flock to the park to relax and have fun. There is no charge for admission to the park or the zoo.

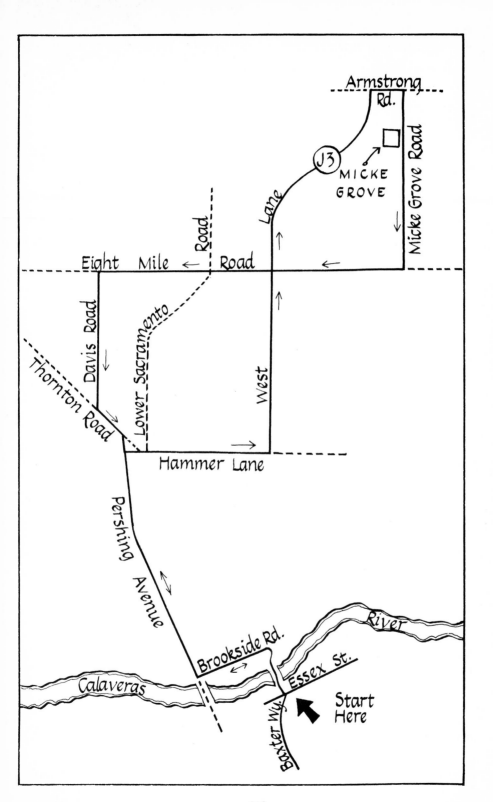

# 45 CAMP RICHARDSON TO FALLEN LEAF LAKE

**General location: South Lake Tahoe**
**Distance: 11.0 miles up and back**
**Riding time: 45 minutes — 1½ hours**
**Road/Traffic conditions: Good/Moderate -
  heavy**
**Facilities: Camp Richardson (June - October)**
**Ride rating: ***

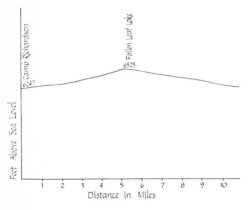

Camp Richardson is located at the southern end of Lake Tahoe near the towns of South Lake Tahoe and Stateline. To reach Camp Richardson take State Highway 89 south from Interstate 80 or north from U.S. 50. Camp Richardson is a popular summer resort operated by the U.S. Forest Service. The headquarters buildings on State Highway 89 are about two long blocks from Lake Tahoe and the beach and boat launching facilities there. From Camp Richardson the route proceeds 0.5 mile north to the turnoff to Fallen Leaf Lake. The ride passes through some heavily wooded areas as the narrow paved road climbs gradually to Fallen Leaf Lake. You will undoubtedly enjoy the fresh scent of pine in the beautifully clear, unsmogged air as you cycle along the Fallen Leaf Road.

Fallen Leaf Lake is a miniature Lake Tahoe. Many comfortable mountain homes rim the edge of the lake's brilliantly clear water. The road to the end of the lake goes along the eastern shore where most of the homes are located, and a beautiful view of much of the lake is available from many vantage points along this route. Several small wooden docks jut out into the lake along the eastern shore and in early season you'll have a great view of a cascading waterfall on the western side of the lake near the Stanford University summer camp.

After you reach the southern end of the lake you will cross a bridge over a gushing mountain stream which empties into the lake. The road turns into a private drive just beyond the bridge so this should be your turning around point.

The return trip to Camp Richardson, since it is mostly downhill, is quick and pleasant. You'll pass the Tahoe Mountain Road turnoff just after leaving the Fallen Leaf Lake area. Although this road connects with Tahoe Boulevard and eventually runs back into State 89 at South Lake Tahoe, it is very rocky and rough. It is not recommended as an alternative circular course back to Camp Richardson.

*Fallen Leaf Lake*

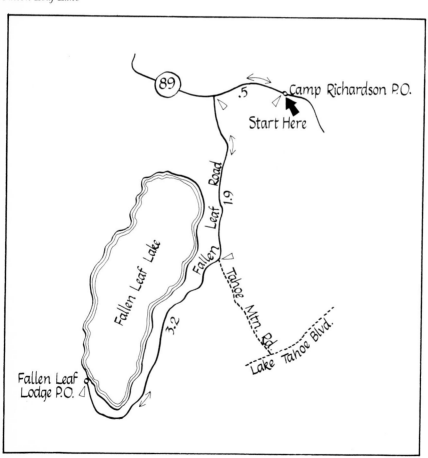

89

.5

Camp Richardson P.O.

Start Here

Fallen Leaf Road

1.9

Fallen Leaf Lake

Tahoe Mtn. Rd.

3.2

Lake Tahoe Blvd.

Fallen Leaf
Lodge P.O.

# 46 HEAVENLY VALLEY TO MEYERS

**General location: South Lake Tahoe**
**Distance: 20 miles round trip**
**Riding time: 1½ - 3 hours**
**Road/Traffic conditions: Very good/Moderate**
**Facilities: South Lake Tahoe, Meyers**
**Ride rating:** * *

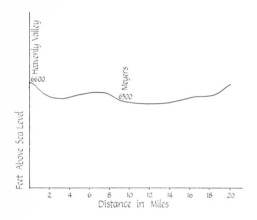

The parking area at the Heavenly Valley Ski Lodge is the pushing off point for this circle ride to Meyers and back via some of Lake Tahoe's scenic back roads. Heavenly Valley can be reached by taking U.S. Highway 50 to Ski Run Boulevard in Stateline. The roadside signs clearly point the way up the hill to the Heavenly Valley Ski Area. From the ski parking area, you will have a breathtaking view of the beautiful waters of Lake Tahoe and the basin around the lake.

The only major hill you will descend and then have to climb back up at the end of the trip is the grade leading from Heavenly Valley. Although this is not a long hill, it is quite steep and may require an alpine gear and/or a little walking on your return. Cycling at Tahoe, either in the spring before the crowds have arrived or in the fall when they have thinned out, can be advantageous. The weather can be a bit unpredictable at these times, but the roads are not as crowded, the accommodations are easier to obtain and the campgrounds are uncrowded. The quiet beauty of the lake is always enjoyable. Stateline, of course, is continually buzzing with gamblers and entertainment seekers, but this trip takes place entirely on the California side and you'll have no need to experience the hustle-bustle of the gambling casinos and stateline traffic.

Sawmill Flat Road, which turns to the left off U.S. 50 near Meyers, is a very quiet, enjoyable part of this ride. The traffic here is very light and the countryside is open in many places, which provides a beautiful view of some of the surrounding mountains and many of the lush green meadows. Although the traffic becomes heavier on Tahoe Boulevard as you move toward Stateline, the roadway is wide and relatively safe. One thing to avoid on Tahoe Boulevard, however, are the drainage grates on the side of the road. These grates are not structured to prevent narrow ten-speed bicycle tires from falling through. Getting your wheel wedged in one of these could result in personal injury as well as damage to tires, wheels, and spokes.

Be sure to turn right off Tahoe Boulevard at Happy Home Cemetery Road. There is also a sign there reading "Lake Tahoe School District Office." You'll angle right almost immediately on Al Tahoe Boulevard on your return ride to the Heavenly Valley Ski Area.

*Historic site near Myers*

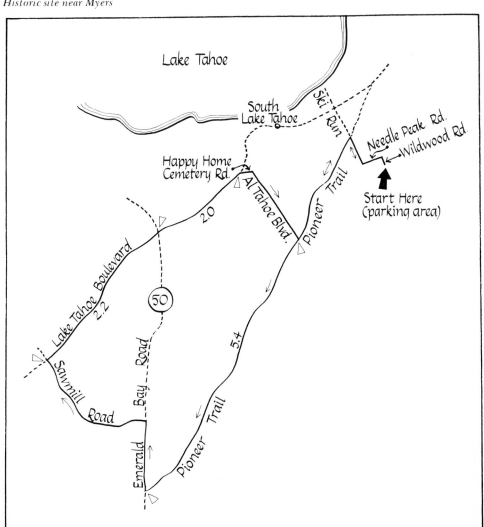

Lake Tahoe

South
Lake Tahoe

Ski Run

Needle Peak Rd.
Wildwood Rd.

Happy Home
Cemetery Rd.

Al Tahoe Blvd.

Pioneer Trail

Start Here
(parking area)

Lake Tahoe Boulevard

2.0

50

2.2

Sawmill Road

Bay Road

5.4

Emerald

Pioneer Trail

# 47 COLUMBIA STATE HISTORIC PARK

**General location: Sonora, east of Stockton**
**Distance: 5.2 miles round trip**
**Riding time: 30 - 45 minutes**
**Road/Traffic conditions: Very good/Light - moderate**
**Facilities: Columbia**
**Ride rating: ***

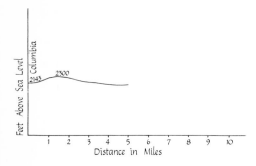

The little gold rush town of Columbia, located only four miles north of Sonora, is a beautifully restored example of what California mining towns were like in the mid 1800's. To reach Columbia take State Highway 49 north (Washington Street) from Sonora for two miles, then turn right on State Highway 4 for two more miles.

Columbia, at 2143 feet in elevation, is in the middle of California's gold country among the rugged hills which were carefully combed by fortune seekers in the 1850's and 1860's. This is a short, easy circle trip on some of the quaint backroads around Columbia.

In 1945 the state started buying property in Columbia so that the buildings still standing there could be renovated to their original gold rush style. One reason that Columbia was an ideal choice for a state historic park depicting early California was that the buildings in the town were made from brick and were still in relatively good condition. The town had been destroyed by two fires in the 1850's and in the third rebuilding, brick was used extensively. The complete destruction by fire of the wood and canvas structures in early gold rush towns was a common occurrence in the Mother Lode Country.

Many of Columbia's old shops and buildings have been recreated. The main street is closed to automobile traffic (open to pedestrians, cyclists and stage coach only). You'll see many of these shops by strolling down the boardwalks or riding along the shady main street. The blacksmith's shop, pharmacy, Wells Fargo Office and woodworker's shop are but a few examples of the superb restoration in the town. Some places of business are open for actual trade. Activities in the Park include picnicking, photography, self-guided tours using the free Columbia State Historic Park brochure map available at the museum, and, of course, cycling.

In the early days Columbia was incredibly rich. First known as Hildreth's Diggin's and American Camp, Columbia had $87 million in gold taken from the area in the 1850's and 1860's. It all started with the gathering of 30 lbs. of nuggets in two days by a group of miners in 1850. During the zenith of Columbia's prosperity (population 10,000) this impressive list of commercial enterprises existed: 4 banks, 3 express offices, 40 saloons, 6 breweries, 8 hotels, 2 fire companies, 3 churches, 2 bookstores, 1 school, 3 theatres (including one Chinese), 53 stores and 150 gambling places.

By 1870 the gold around Columbia had disappeared and what was left of the town was an empty shell, a ghost town. But the restored town today and your imagination can vividly recreate this quaint little town into what she was once called — "Gem of the Southern Mines."

*Main Street in Columbia*

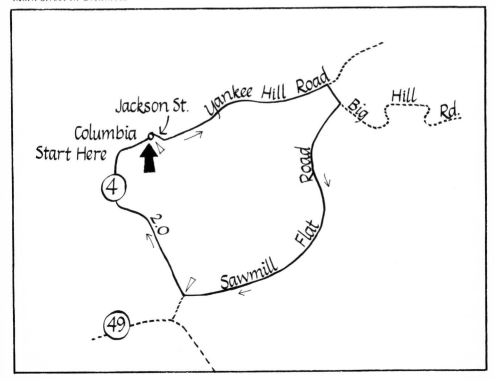

Jackson St.

Yankee Hill Road

Big Hill Rd.

Columbia
Start Here

4

2.0

Road

Flat

Sawmill

49

# 48 SONORA CIRCLE RIDE

**General location: Sonora**
**Distance: 10.4 miles round trip**
**Riding time: 1 - 2½ hours**
**Road/Traffic conditions: Very good/Moderate**
**Facilities: Sonora**
**Ride rating: **

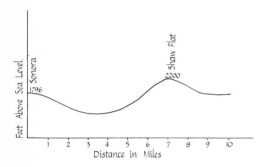

To reach the town of Sonora, the starting place for this ride, take State Highways 120 and 108 east to State Highway 49 which goes north through Sonora. This ride, although it is not a long one, is rated two stars because of one quite long and challenging hill on Shaw's Flat Jamestown Road. Other than this stretch of road the first and last few miles of the trip from Sonora and back into Sonora are downhill. The ride up Shaw Flat Jamestown Road is quiet and picturesque and the level meadowlands at the top of the road at Shaw Flat make for enjoyable cycling. The ride down Highway 49 and North Washington Street through Sonora is also interesting and most pleasant. You will pass by many of the old buildings in Sonora as you coast through the town.

Sonora has maintained its early day characteristics as a hustle-bustle little town in spite of the fact that the gold rush days were over 100 years ago. Since Sonora is built in a rather hilly area, many of the side streets are narrow and steep. The town's main street (Washington) will offer you a good view of many of the older buildings — the courthouse, county library, the red Victorian Gunter house, and lovely old St. James Episcopal church.

When her mines were closed Sonora turned to cattle and lumbering and now is an important crossroads and gateway for tourists traveling through the Mother Lode Country.

The Sonora of gold rush days had a population of more than 14,000 at one time and mined a large share of the $600 million in gold taken from Tuolumne County mines (including one nugget weighing over 28 lbs.) Although gutted by fire four times in three years, Sonora always bounced back to become a sophisticated, cosmopolitan gold mining town. Crystal chandeliered saloons served liquid refreshments chilled by snow packed down from the Sierra while velvet-clad women sang for the customers. Bull and bear fights, traveling circuses, and roving minstrels provided street entertainment in those bawdy early days.

If you have time, a visit to the Tuolumne County museum might be worthwhile. The museum, located on West Bradford Street in the 106 year old jail contains many historical items pertinent to Sonora including many old photos. The museum is open 9-12 and 1-5 daily in the summer and Monday through Friday the rest of the year.

*Gunter House in Sonora*

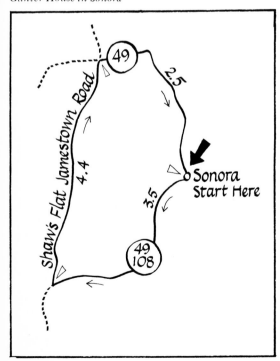

# 49  ANGELS CAMP TO MURPHYS

**General location:** Sonora
**Distance:** 16.5 miles round trip
**Riding time:** 1½ - 2 hours
**Road/Traffic conditions:** Very good/Moderate
**Facilities:** Angels Camp; Murphys
**Ride rating:** ★★

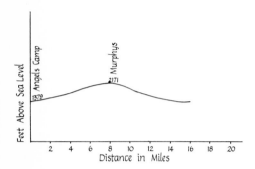

Angels Camp, annual site of the famous Calaveras County frog jumping contest, is the picturesque setting for the start of this delightful ride. Angels Camp is about 17 miles north of Sonora on State Highway 49. This circle route to Murphys and back goes through some very beautiful, hilly ranch country. The ride from Angels Camp to Murphys is a steady but gradual uphill grade but, of course, what goes up must come down; from Murphys back to Angels Camp you'll experience an exhilarating downhill trip along cascading Angels Creek.

The town of Angels Camp was founded by George Angel in 1848 when he discovered gold here. He later started the town's first trading post and gave the town its name. Mr. Angel prospered as the town boomed during the gold rush. He sold ordinary shirts for $50 and tools for up to $200 each. Although Angels Camp was big and rich for a time it inevitably faded when the gold supply dwindled. But the little town was made immortal by two authors, Mark Twain and Bret Harte, who frequented this area in the late 1800's. Twain is famous for his story entitled "The Celebrated Jumping Frog of Calaveras County" which he supposedly heard from a bartender at the Angels Hotel.

The old town of Murphys is one of the most quaint, well preserved Mother Lode towns in the gold country. Many stone structures were built in Murphys because of fires which destroyed much of the town in 1859, 1874 and 1893. Many of the buildings along the main street are from the 1850's, the most prominent being the Murphys Hotel, which has a large bar and a dining hall that serves as the town's social center on Saturday nights. Also in the Hotel is a reproduction of the register showing the names of Charles Bolton (Black Bart), Mark Twain, Horatio Alger, Ulysses S. Grant and others. If you're interested in taking a look, just ask the barkeep.

Murphys was settled in 1848 by John and Daniel Murphy who came west in 1844 on the first immigrant train to California. They made their fortunes in gold and then ran a very successful trading post, which sometimes took as much as $400 a day in gold dust. Their town prospered with more than $15 million in gold being shipped by Wells Fargo in less than 10 years. At its peak, Murphys had a population of 5,000, a cider and syrup factory, a bowling alley and eight busy taverns.

If you reach Murphys on a warm day and hanker for a place to cool your heels, you might consider visiting Mercer Caverns. There are guided tours of the 55 degree caves (tour time about 30 minutes) which are well-lighted with good walkways. In the caverns you will see many good examples of stalactites, stalagmites, and helicites. The road to the caverns goes north from the center of town and climbs one mile to the entrance to the caves.

*Jumping Frog Monument*

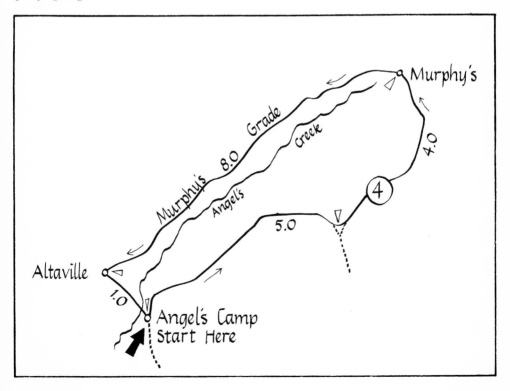

# 50 YOSEMITE VALLEY

General location: Yosemite National Park, Yosemite Valley
Distance: 16.5 miles round trip
Riding time: 1½ - 2½ hours
Road/Traffic conditions: Very good/Moderate - heavy
Facilities: Yosemite Village
Ride rating: **

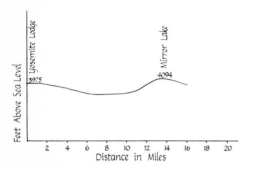

There are three access routes to Yosemite Valley: State Highway 120 through the Big Oak Flat entrance from the north, State Highway 140 from Merced, Mariposa, and El Portal from the west, and Highway 41 from the south.

Biking in Yosemite provides a superb, unobstructed view of the natural beauty of the Valley. Cycling in this spectacular area is growing dramatically in popularity and will undoubtedly continue to grow in future years as automobile traffic is diminished and other forms of transportation encouraged. By 1980 the U.S. Department of the Interior has estimated that without changes, over a million cars will jam into the valley. That is why a scenic, one-way route has been established on the valley floor and shuttle bus service to all facilities in the upper valley has begun. Signs stating that bikes and cars have equal rights on the roadways in the valley also is an encouragement to and a reinforcement of the basic rights of the cyclist. Eventually, when all automobile traffic is eliminated, the valley will become an even more idyllic place for the cyclist to enjoy the unsurpassed beauty of Yosemite.

Except for the short hill to Mirror Lake, this trip's entire 16.5 mile loop is on the valley floor and is therefore, very level. A crossover road from Northside to Southside Drive exists near El Capitan for cyclists who either choose not to or are unable to complete the full loop. A bikeway, completely closed to motorized traffic, is available at the upper end of the valley near Mirror Lake. This short, serene route in the shadow of Half Dome (8842') goes past the Indian Caves, over Sugarpine Bridge and past the Ahwahnee Hotel. This route will give you some idea of what the entire valley will be like eventually.

Park Rangers have started to conduct "handlebar ecology trips" in the park which are an informative and leisurely way to become acquainted with the park and accustomed to cycling on valley roads. Rangers usually start these two-hour, four-mile bicycle tours from the Yosemite Lodge bike rental area. Fluorescent vests are loaned to each participant for the duration of the tour. On the tour you may learn something about the geology of the valley, the early history of the park, or stop to view some of the daring climbers scaling the precarious face of El Capitan (7569'). The trips are usually taken at a very slow pace with plenty of time for sightseeing, listening and asking of questions.

There is a very short little side trip on Northside Drive just as you begin to pass El Capitan. This one-lane, one-way road which goes to the right passes even more closely to the smooth granite face of El Capitan. It is a road traveled mainly by climbers preparing to ascend the rock and offers an excellent view of the forehead and nose of the "Captain" as well as closeup of any climbers who might be preparing to go climbing.

On Southside Drive you will pass by a right hand turnoff to beautiful Bridalveil Fall, then past the majestic Cathedral Rocks and Sentinel Dome. In the area near Sentinel Dome you will be able to get a good view of Yosemite Falls on the northern side of the valley. The route you will follow to complete the entire loop turns right toward Curry Village just before crossing Sentinel Bridge and reaching Yosemite Village. Much of this loop in the upper end of the valley is closed to automobile traffic so it is very safe for cycling. Mirror Lake at the extreme eastern end of the valley is a small, pretty body of water which is a very popular visiting place for shuttle buses, hikers and bicyclists. After descending the hill from Mirror Lake you'll turn right toward the Indian Caves, pass through Yosemite Village and return to Yosemite Lodge with its spectacular view of Yosemite Falls.

Yosemite offers a variety of activities and things to see. Besides cycling there are naturalist programs, hiking, climbing, riding, fishing, swimming, skiing and camping only to name a few. Consult the park literature or the park information service for further details.

*Handlebar Ecology Trip near El Capitan*

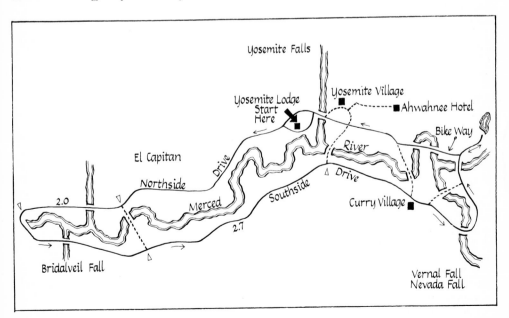

*Old house near Columbia State Park*

Photos on pages
13, 22, 49, 65, 68, 96, 97
by Bob Oswald

*Editor*
   *Thomas K. Worcester*
*Design*
   *T. E. Sadler*